Being Ourself

Ty Clement

First published by O Books, 2009
O Books is an imprint of John Hunt Publishing Ltd., The Bothy, Deershot Lodge, Park Lane, Ropley, Hants, SO24 0BE, UK
office1@o-books.net
www.o-books.net

Distribution in:	South Africa
	Alternative Books
UK and Europe	altbook@peterhyde.co.za
.Orca Book Services	Tel: 021 555 4027 Fax: 021 447 1430
orders@orcabookservices.co.uk	
Tel: 01202 665432 Fax: 01202 666219	Text copyright Ty Clement 2008
Int. code (44)	
	Design: Stuart Davies
USA and Canada	
NBN	ISBN: 978 1 84694 182 5
custserv@nbnbooks.com	
Tel: 1 800 462 6420 Fax: 1 800 338 4550	All rights reserved. Except for brief quotations in critical articles or reviews, no part of this
	book may be reproduced in any manner without
Australia and New Zealand	prior written permission from the publishers.
Brumby Books	
. sales@brumbybooks.com.au	The rights of Ty Clement as author have been
Tel: 61 3 9761 5535 Fax: 61 3 9761 7095	asserted in accordance with the Copyright,
	Designs and Patents Act 1988.
Far East (offices in Singapore, Thailand,	
Hong Kong, Taiwan)	
Pansing Distribution Pte Ltd	
kemal@pansing.com	A CIP catalogue record for this book is available
Tel: 65 6319 9939 Fax: 65 6462 5761	from the British Library.

Printed by Digital Book Print

O Books operates a distinctive and ethical publishing philosophy in all areas of its business, from its global network of authors to production and worldwide distribution.
This book is produced on FSC certified stock, within ISO14001 standards. The printer plants sufficient trees each year through· the Woodland Trust to absorb the level of emitted carbon in its production.

Being
Ourself

Ty Clement

BOOKS

Winchester, UK
Washington, USA

CONTENTS

Dedication

This book is dedicated to my lovely and amazing wife, Sara, who made important contributions to this project every step of the way and supported me unconditionally, and to my beautiful mother, Jill, who taught me kindness, love, and compassion through her incredible example.

Acknowledgments

I would like to express the deepest gratitude to my five sons whose special combination of humour, creativity, and wisdom keeps me in my place, and fills me with constant wonder and love. Thank you also to my brothers in life who have supported me in so many important ways: Ed Clement, Ted Clement, Michael Miracle, Chris Murray, John Monroe, Hans Cavins, John Gorringe, Antonio, Eric Sells, Paul Sells, Jim Zhang, Matt Schehl, Dave Browder, Bill Walsh, Ruslan Henderson, Dave Brown, Daniel Potter, and the Voodoo Horseshoes.

Additional thanks to Amy Ratto-Parks for your support and literary expertise, and to John Hunt and everyone else at O-Books, a company with real vision. Thank you also to all my brothers and sisters in the Being Ourself group on beliefnet.com for being Ourself!

Last but not least, thank you Elmira Ingersoll for encouraging me in such a sincere and timely way; I can't express how important that was to me.

Invitation

Introducing...Ourself

This is a book about Ourself. What do we mean by Ourself? Ourself is the one thing that *is*—everybody and everything, everywhere, as an absolute whole. Grammatically speaking, "our" is supposed to be followed by the plural "selves" because the English language presumes that "our" as a possessive adjective refers to ownership by a group of *intrinsically separate* individuals. Though we appear separate as we move about with seeming independence, a more comprehensive look reveals that all creatures and objects are like the teeth of a comb which appear separate along one side, but can clearly be seen to be different parts of the same one thing when viewed as a whole.

The tragic consequence of our language's grammatical assumption of separateness is that we have a difficult time recognizing that one's primary identity is not as a separate individual, but rather as an indivisible aspect of reality itself. Therefore, "our" in its most fundamental sense should be followed by the singular "self" since "our" taken to its broadest and most inclusive extreme refers to our fundamental identity, reality, as a singular whole. This all-inclusive identity might initially seem abstract or irrelevant, but by deeply and feelingly penetrating the illusion of separateness which most of us live our lives bound within, we burst into a vastness of being, understanding, and guidance unlike anything available within the isolating "me, myself, and I" framework of thought.

Referring to all of creation with a singular title such as "Ourself" is an important step towards making this understanding more widely accessible. True spiritual freedom is freedom from the sensation of the self as an isolated identity. We become exposed to this freedom anytime our listening and

1

looking wander beyond the realm of thought and into the depths of reality itself; allowing us to recognize first hand that in the most basic sense reality is *one thing* manifested into an infinite variety of forms interacting with itself. Discovering relief from the brain's persistent muscular assertion of the narrow and limiting construct of "me, myself, and I" by merely permitting our awareness to reach a little further into the natural wholeness of *everything* is as monumental an experience as a chick breaking out of its eggshell and entering the world as an active and inseparable part of creation. No matter how many radically different forms existence takes or makes, existence as a whole remains one entity that we all come from, and are all part of.

This singular ultimate identity includes both the *source* and the *substance* of reality. In other words the Creator and creation are inseparable, and we are each inextricably part of this whole. This absolute whole of source and substance has been called by many different names, such as God, the Tao, Allah, or Brahman, but the reality remains the same no matter how people label it or define it. The details of what the source and substance of all things is precisely like can be discovered uniquely by each of us, and celebrated within whatever cultural context we choose. However, the critical universal truth that transcends details of belief and culture is that, whether we like it or not, we are all inescapably different parts of one whole interacting with itself—or more accurately, Ourself.

Rather than continuing to waste energy and lives fighting throughout the world over whose version of God or reality is correct, it is urgent that we begin to acknowledge that no matter what nationality or culture we are part of we share the same core identity as aspects of reality itself. The goal of this book is neither to prove nor disprove any particular belief, but instead to open the way for us all to begin witnessing our common nature as inseparable parts *of nature*. I have offered the name "Ourself" for this fundamentally common identity we are all branches of because of the word's implication of ultimate inclusiveness, but it is not the particular name that is important. What *is* important is that we at least begin to develop a more inclusive language of spirituality if we are ever to move beyond the dangerous state of fragmentation that our currently limited language constantly reinforces.

Using exclusively individualistic language in our conception of ourselves and the universe not only blinds us to the underlying wholeness of Ourself, but also to the compassion and ecstasy to be found in this wholeness. Though our bodies appear to be separate autonomous entities, they are in fact indivisible aspects of the whole of physical reality. Food, water, and air literally become our bodies; and similarly our wastes (and eventually our whole bodies) rejoin the solids, liquids, and gases of our surroundings. By recognizing that our bodies appear separate but are actually molded streams of the same "reality-stuff" as everything else, we can begin to realize that spiritually we are similarly indivisible aspects of the total consciousness of everything.

Entering this all inclusive consciousness of Ourself is the "on" switch to our real spiritual lives because it is only through listening beyond the clamor of "me, myself, and I," and thereby recognizing that we are merely parts of one whole, that we can truly relax into the vastness of Spirit. This is equally true whether we consider ourselves to be spiritual, religious, agnostic, or even atheist. The genuine enlightenment and meaning we ultimately crave and need is making the acquaintance of the simple essential nature we all share, and realizing that this absolutely common nature, Ourself, is who we really are.

With a wealth of peace, fulfillment, and beauty so readily available to us through the simple recognition that our assumption of separateness is unfounded, why do we remain so committed to the delusion of separateness? The image of the donkey that merely marches forward in pursuit of the carrot that has been hung in front of it without ever critically analyzing the futility of such a pursuit appears to be part of the answer to this question. The blind assumption that we are all separate entities is the bedrock of the persistent dialogue of "me, myself, and I" which our verbally mechanical thinking drones on with endlessly. Our thinking does not like interruptions or challenges to the validity of this endless dialogue; we like to take "me, myself, and I" very seriously.

In addition to this inertia that keeps us spellbound by the "me, myself, and I" carrot of thought, our minds also seem to prefer to believe in inherently separate identities because through this denial of the oneness of all things we are freed from meaningful consideration of our relationships and responsibilities to other people, the environment, and Ourself as a whole. Our thinking therefore finds the profound implications which emerge in the light of Ourself to be quite threatening. Not only are our minds resistant to the inconvenience of our innate sense of responsibility to each other as different aspects of the same one thing, but we are also afraid of losing individual identity, control, and autonomy. Yet, in truth, this fundamental fear of losing personal control is unfounded.

In acknowledging that we are all ultimately parts of one whole we don't give up or lose any part of ourselves as individuals—we instead gain a clearer awareness of who we really are by seeing ourselves within the transformative, holistic framework of Ourself. Being Ourself is not the cessation of individuality, it is the recognition that our individuality is inseparably embedded in the context of reality as a whole, which is one thing interacting with itself.

In other words, just because our fundamental identity is Ourself, it doesn't mean we have lost our secondary identities as individuals. In being Ourself we never stop being "me, John Doe" or "me, Jane Doe." We instead retain all of our individual and unique qualities and powers while simultaneously beginning to develop an understanding of how they fit into the big picture of everyone and everything else's unique qualities and powers.

While understanding that we are all truly one *does* awaken our sense of compassion for all living creatures and for Ourself as a whole, this does not compromise our ability to fulfill our own individual, family, or community needs. Unfortunately, however, our self-centered minds perceive and fear this holistic awareness as the ultimate "buzz-kill." We don't want to be bothered with the profound implications of oneness. We want the "freedom" to be completely absorbed in our own preferences and scheming— but is this really "freedom?" How does it really feel to be completely consumed with our own thinking? Isn't it more like answering to a slave driver than being free? Aren't the petulant demands of the "me" monologue in our heads ultimately exhausting and painful?

What would it be like to be aware of our own thought monologues in a way similar to a wise and grounded elder being aware of the chatter and whining of his or her grandchildren— not ignoring them, and not discounting them, but also not obsessively trying to please their every whim! Can we be aware of our thinking concurrently with our awareness of everything else within us and around us? Can we dwell in the quiet and majesty of Ourself as we hear out the gnawing consideration that our minds engage in endlessly?

If we can, we will begin to know real inner peace. Inner peace is no more the cessation of thought than peace for the elder would be the cessation of her or his grandchildren's enthusiastic chatter. We come to know enduring inner peace through being aware of vastly more of what we are than just our thinking, our opinions, our beliefs, and our preferences. As we allow our awareness to deepen and broaden beyond the narrow realm of "me, myself, and I" we become aware of the infinite and eternal quality of Ourself that permeates all that is within and without. This awareness has a cooling and calming effect on our minds in a way similar to the cooling and calming effect that the elder's grounded and quiet wisdom have on his or her grandchildren.

In contrast, deep within our thoughts and feelings most of us are haunted by a sense of uneasiness and irritability that is the consequence of our absolute commitment to maintaining the mirage of separateness. We settle for terms like "interconnected" as a way of superficially acknowledging that all phenomena are at least related to each other in one way or another, but we as a culture have really not begun to acknowledge that we are much more than merely interconnected—we literally are *one thing* interacting with Ourself.

Throughout human history, and especially so today, the artificial divisions humans have so passionately created and upheld between individuals, families, communities, cultures, religions, and nationalities have been responsible for completely tragic and unnecessary suffering, violence, and destruction to human, animal, and plant life. It is the shared responsibility of us all to end this insanity; not by ending or denying our differences, but instead by acknowledging the superficiality of our differences in comparison to the profundity of our oneness.

If we refrain from naming something we deny it, or hide from it. Acknowledging the singular nature of reality with a word that conveys ultimate inclusivity and ultimate oneness might be the critical step we need to take if we are ever to experience real peace individually, collectively, and internationally. Though many words in different languages are synonymous with Ourself, most of these words have become focal points of conflict between different cultures or religions. The word Ourself is not meant to replace each culture's or individual's preferred word for ultimate reality, but instead to provide a generic word for members of any culture or religion to share that is so inclusive and simplistic that it eliminates conflicts by offering a neutral common denominator. Clearly today's polarized and violent world is in desperate need of this neutrality and commonality.

We each make a choice in every moment of our lives, whether

consciously or unconsciously, to either recognize ourselves as parts of the whole, or to instead cling to the appearance of separateness. In other words, we can choose to recklessly criticize or discount the value of looking deeper into what we are, and seeing the big picture. We can tell ourselves that oneness is some unattainable state of consciousness that requires a lifetime of rigid spiritual practice or of disciplined study of Eastern religions. Similarly, we can hold others up as being enlightened messiahs as a way of excusing ourselves from having to step into every moment with the sometimes overwhelming, but always miraculous, awareness that we are all Ourself.

In contrast, we can choose to innocently and enthusiastically embrace our true identity, Ourself, and allow our lives to take shape and evolve out of this broad and open feeling. This book will guide you through a series of "Reflections," which appear as an italicized passage in each chapter, to help you begin to recognize and experience this broad and open feeling, and to help you begin the journey of manifesting your unique talents and gifts as Ourself. The slower you move through these Reflections, the more you will get out of (or *get into*) them. As you make your way through each Reflection, stop reading as often as you need to give yourself time to feel and reflect.

The same holds true for reading the book in general—if you read too much too fast you risk getting bogged down in the words, and the repetitious nature of the message. Take little bites, chew them well, and really savor the taste of each bite. Nourishing our awareness and experience of Ourself is a lot like nourishing our bodies; it isn't an intellectual affair. Eating itself is a repetitive process (don't we all sometimes just get sick of having to prepare food and having to eat?), and once we are overly full the food we are eating stops tasting good. Approach the reading slowly, let your demanding intellect take a break, and focus on tasting and experiencing the richness of the reality the words urgently attempt to convey—a magical, wondrous, and all-inclusive reality which has been so powerfully yet silently denied.

One of the most tragic results of both our resistance to acknowledging the sacred oneness of all things, and the absence of an adequate word in our language to describe this oneness, has been the alienation of so many young people from spirituality in general. When all that is offered to young people is a contrived portrayal of the "Creator" as a white haired, elderly, Caucasian stud clothed skimpily in a pair of glowing men's briefs, floating in some distant clouds "up there," the result is a generation who often fails to realize that just because this picture of the ultimate source of reality is obviously fatally incomplete, it doesn't mean that an ultimate source or spiritual dimension to reality doesn't exist at all.

In truth, we can know intimately the source of reality because it is synonymous with the substance of reality that we too are part of—the source and the substance are both aspects of the whole of Ourself. Why not offer this accurate and accessible understanding of the nature of reality to our young people? How might we all have benefited if this vision of reality had been offered to us throughout our lives, and allowed us to creatively grow and develop with a sense of wholeness and validation rooted in reality itself?

My hope is for the widespread acknowledgment of Ourself to begin to melt away all conceptual walls and barriers amongst ourselves, and between human beings and our source. I hope for the word Ourself to illuminate to humankind as a whole that *everything everywhere* is actually *one* thing; creating a flood of awareness that flushes out every last trace of the chilling and sinister sensation of separateness that so many people feel between themselves and other people, and between themselves and their source. I hope for Ourself to become a word that all people come to recognize and understand through their own unique experience of the one reality that we are all part of; marking an end to the destructive consensual divisions which now exist both within humanity, and between humans and nature.

Ourself is not a word which separates or segregates as the many different words for "God" have done. It is a word which anybody can use to refer to the one deep truth which we are all unique aspects of. Ourself can not alienate, or mislead, as it is the most inclusive word imaginable. It does not conflict with the views of any group or culture because its meaning has no boundaries or dogma. It merely refers to reality as a whole—all that exists in this world and any other world which happens to exist, be it physical or spiritual. It can be likened to the area where many circles overlap—it is the essential bare truth which conflicts with nothing because it is in fact everything.

If we remain rigidly attached to words and concepts that are specific to our own particular religion or subculture, then we keep the one reality that we are all part of unavailable to ourselves and humanity as a whole. Consciousness of this one reality we are all part of needs to be shared by humankind in spite of our many religious and ethnic differences. A powerful animosity has grown through the ages between religions and cultures with different names for the ultimate source and substance of reality, and the historical result has too often been horrific acts of violence.

The simplicity and generality of the word Ourself leaves each of us the space to see and interpret the reality that we are all part of for ourselves without requiring us to agree upon the details. In this way the word Ourself is similar to the number zero—it is more like a non-symbol than a symbol. It is like a transparent map that allows you to see the actual landscape through it; a word with such an invisible meaning that it leaves the mind free to simply see reality as it is.

The introduction of such a boundless and inclusive word creates an opening in our language. The word Ourself acts like a vacuum—its infinite width, and utter lack of specificity, draws all

words which do specify into itself, like fish into the sea. I passionately hope that the introduction of the word Ourself marks the
beginning of a time when all the people of this world understand
together that our common ground as vital and active parts of
creation is much more relevant and important than our differences.

Ourself *is* the "unity in diversity" that this world so desperately needs at this time of international tension and conflict. By
acknowledging Ourself we will be better able to understand how
our differences complement each other rather than degrade each
other. The missing link to our wholeness isn't another little link—
it is the one BIG link that runs through *all* other links, forming the
whole that includes everything and everyone, everywhere. Let's
start *being Ourself!*

Chapter 1

Getting to Know Ourself

Ourself is a word which ultimately has one function—to express the absolutely inclusive nature of reality as a whole. In order to talk about or describe the true context we all exist within as aspects of creation interacting with itself, we need access to words which clearly convey the wondrous indivisibility of everybody and everything. The absence of such vocabulary from the English language up to this point has contributed greatly to humankind's fundamentally common identity remaining an unmentionable secret in our culture. So far the only jargon that has been readily available to us to capture the meaning and implications of a word such as Ourself is that of the Eastern religions; which for many Westerners may feel second hand, unauthentic, or even exclusive.

This is why an original and authentically Western word for the spiritual reality which we are all part of has been so direly needed in our culture. We have excluded our true nature—the source and substance of reality itself—from both our conversations with each other, and from our own thinking as individuals, by altogether failing to name or identify this ultimate identity within our language. Hence, the most obvious thing that we all are—reality itself—has been turned into a subject surrounded by mystique and esoteric charm requiring us to have a guru or spiritual teacher, and some sort of complex meditation practice to recognize. Well, the buck stops here. Let's be perfectly clear with ourselves once and for all—*we are all* Ourself interacting with Ourself, and we all have equal opportunity for insight into our universal identity because reality itself is neither Eastern nor Western!

When we begin to experience reality directly, letting go of all that we have ever been told or taught that reality is, we start really getting to know Ourself. Getting to know Ourself is the ongoing discovery of who and what we actually are. In order to begin this process we need to first recognize that there is no concrete or isolated "me" residing in any individual's consciousness; we are each moving collages of different thoughts, impressions, strivings, and desires which have no exact center and no exact outer limit. Though we tend to think of ourselves as completely separate and contained entities, the entire human race is actually no more than a web of processes within the total process of everything, everywhere. When we recognize that everything in reality is an extension of the same one thing, then we realize that our true identity has no walls, ceiling, floor, or core to it.

Unlocking your car door with the key, you see all the locks inside the car pop into the unlocked position. When you recognize that everything is one thing interacting with itself, a similar unlocking action occurs throughout your being—somehow everything instantly feels different, and reality takes on a brighter look. This is the real Wonderland, Narnia, or Hogwarts! The transformation of our experience of reality when we first truly recognize that what we have perceived to be a universe of completely separate components is actually one thing interacting with itself in the form of *apparently* separate components, is just as magnificent and mind-blowing a transformation as stumbling into another world through the looking glass, the back of the wardrobe, or platform nine and three quarters.

This insight into the common nature of ourselves and reality dislodges our stuck feelings and assumptions which both stem from and sustain the static sensation of "I," or "me." All sensation of self as separate gets washed into the one *whole* experience of reality as Ourself. It's like stirring the dry and crusty cake batter from the upper edges of a mixing bowl, where it has bunched up and stuck, back into the smooth wet batter, integrating it with the whole. While this first squeegee-ing of the upper crusty edges of the mixing bowl of our consciousness with the spatula of insight feels incredibly wonderful, and leaves us with an initial taste of how it feels to be absolutely *with* and *of* everything, we soon find that this is only the beginning of a lifelong rhythmic process of remembering and forgetting.

The production factory of the convincing illusion of separateness that constantly brings about this forgetting is a combination of our psychological capacity to identify and label things as separate with our psychological capacity to attach meaning and feelings to each identity and label. This process is like a jelly donut machine where the separate identities and labels are the basic bland donuts, and the meanings and emotions we associate with each identity and label become the flavorful jelly of feeling which brings to life in our consciousness the sensation that each identity and label is a completely separate entity. Each of these jelly donuts in our consciousness is a stored image that we psychologically relate to as innately separate, and therefore reinforces the overall feeling that reality is a collection of plainly individual parts.

As soon as we have begun producing and collecting these jelly donuts in our consciousness as children we have developed the capacity for "us versus them" thinking and feeling, and we are well on our way to feeling separate by nature from the rest of reality. The problem is not that we have the capacity to distinguish and name different aspects of reality; the problem is that we seem to lack the capacity to keep sight of life's wholeness in the process. We rapidly become completely alienated from Ourself by the disorienting jelly donuts that endlessly pile up in our consciousness. So how do we neutralize the disorienting effect of the jelly donuts, and become reacquainted with Ourself? There is nothing we can do from the disoriented mindset of separateness to free ourselves from the vast collection of jelly donuts we have constructed in our consciousness because the director of all such self-help or psychological efforts, "me, myself, and I" is a jelly donut itself!

The only lasting relief we can find from the stifling pile of jelly donuts that has obscured our true identity is to awaken the mighty, jelly donut munching dragon, Ourself, from its lengthy slumber. Reality itself is the intelligence which is able to see through the façade of separateness which each jelly donut of our mind spins. When our thoughts and feelings become exposed to the profound brilliance of reality's absolute wholeness, the persuasive illusiveness of our thoughts and feelings begins to weaken, and we become conscious that we are actually life being aware of life. As reality, the jelly donut munching dragon, begins to digest all the jelly donuts of our mind, their disorienting effect is neutralized. We are freed from the stifling illusion of separateness, and we find ourselves face to face with Ourself.

While this initial re-acquaintance is certainly powerful and transformative, we sometimes place too much emphasis on these initial "spiritual experiences." We easily forget that the rest of our lives lay ahead, and if we are to remain truly conscious of our identity as part of the great wholeness, then ongoing cleansing of the static and sticky sensation of separateness will be required. In other words, it's not that you will ever be able to stop your mind and heart from building a momentum of alienation through the constant production of jelly donuts, but rather that you will develop an everlasting practice of dispersing this momentum through your awareness of Ourself which can digest each donut as it comes along.

This is the essence of self-awareness and self-honesty—not merely being aware of and honest with ourselves about what we think and feel as individuals, but being aware of and honest with ourselves about our infinite and eternal identity. This involves really getting to know all the aspects of ourselves that we consider separate (our body, our thoughts, and our feelings) as different parts of the same one thing. Our consciousness, including all our thoughts and feelings, is like an inverted chunk of reality that doesn't recognize itself. Nothing within us is in any way separate from the rest of reality which we experience as being "outside" of ourselves. Everybody and everything, including all of our thoughts and feelings, all exist within and are part of the same house. Moving out of our messy, poster-clad bedroom with the dirty laundry of isolation littered all over the floor, and checking out the magnificent house as a whole is getting to know Ourself.

No matter how isolated, selfish, or noxious we might feel, all of this isolation, selfishness, and noxiousness when unveiled turn out to be nothing more than reality experiencing itself in the form of thought. When we can admit to ourselves that our entire thinking and feeling experience of, "me, myself, and I" is actually nothing more than Ourself experiencing itself as thought and feeling, the "me" bubble bursts, and the pressure and pain of isolation begins to disperse. Bathing in our newfound awareness of Ourself is the most therapeutic and renewing experience available anywhere, and we don't have to wait for some special ritualized time or place to experience this renewal and healing because Ourself is everywhere all the time!

We have become accustomed to hearing things like, "we are all interconnected," and we can stomach that sentiment easily enough because it doesn't threaten our sense of individuality or individual control. However, seeing ourselves and the rest of reality as one holistic identity takes the sentiment of "we are all interconnected" to another level—one that we tend to be very resistant to, and uncomfortable with. We may therefore find ourselves tempted to belittle, laugh at, or make fun of such declarations of ultimate oneness. We don't want to think of ourselves as tentacles on some sort of massive, all encompassing one-thing-centipede! It makes us feel out of control—we fear that we will lose our unique identities, and our freewill.

However, whether we *want* to see it or *not*, we *are* merely Ourself. Making fun of, or avoiding the truth doesn't make it disappear; burying our heads in the sand is not a productive way of dealing with our fear of being engulfed or absorbed by the great wholeness. The only productive way of dealing with this fear is to look right into it, and to see that the fear itself is only another face of Ourself.

In reality, we don't lose anything by acknowledging or seeing the truth that we are only parts of the whole. Ourself doesn't engulf or absorb us, and we don't lose any of our uniqueness in recognizing that fundamentally we are all reality interacting with itself. Actually it is only through this recognition that we gain the enlightening holistic awareness of Ourself which helps us to better recognize our unique talents and qualities, and to better manifest these talents and qualities as individuals.

This is like the difference between seeing each of your fingers as separate entities poking out of little holes in a big black mitten, versus seeing the whole of your hand with all five fingers attached. Our fingers are not just "interconnected," they are all literally of one hand! Seeing the whole picture of all five fingers as part of one hand allows you to understand how each finger as part of the hand helps the whole to function; the unique roles of each finger become clearer, not cloudier. The same is true of becoming aware of ourselves as unique parts of Ourself.

Think about trying to play the piano if each of our fingers could only follow its own individual impulses, as opposed to all of our fingers working as a whole to create beautiful music. This isn't to say that we can all simply be played by Ourself like the fingers of a hand, but in a very real way reality is coordinated as a whole. By being aware of our individual selves as Ourself we become available participants in this subtle, but infinitely sublime, coordinated pattern of change which is the constant motion of everything's eternal state of becoming.

Looking at the evolution of science, mathematics, or art, one can see these patterns of interactivity and synchronicity at work. Similarly, if you look back at the course of your entire life, you can see how a pattern of connect-the-dot-like experiences has created the shape of your life as a whole. You can also see how meaningfully interactive your life has been with the lives of others. The Christmas classic, *It's a Wonderful Life*, does a remarkable job illustrating this when George Bailey is given the chance to see what the lives of the people in his hometown would have looked like had he never been born. Again, it may not be as simple or obvious as the fingers of our hand playing the piano, but by being conscious of Ourself we will become aware of how our lives can flow forth in a meaningfully informed way, creating new possibilities for productive interactivity and synchronicity with the lives of those around us.

There is nothing more magical or exciting than becoming conscious of this and experiencing your life in this way. Similarly, there is no deeper way to connect with other people than to spontaneously experience Ourself's coordinated process of interactivity. A commonplace example of this kind of experience is when you think of a friend you haven't been in touch with for a while, and then you either get a phone call from the person soon after thinking of them, or maybe you run into the friend while out doing errands. Most of us have probably had much more complex and intense experiences of a similar nature—experiences which verge on the miraculous, and yet also seem completely natural when we are familiar with the mysteriousness of Ourself.

In order to more fully experience our lives in this magical way we need to really get to know Ourself—to see and feel ourselves as Ourself in a deeply kinesthetic or experiential way. We have to start looking not just from our eyes, but from inside our bodies, and outside our bodies simultaneously. We have to be aware of everything we experience as "inside"—our thinking, our heartbeats, our breathing, and our bones—at the same time as we are aware of everything we experience as "outside"—the beautiful, mundane, and ugly sights, sounds, and smells all around us. If we can experience this simultaneous awareness of inner and outer activity, we can see through the illusory line of demarcation our minds draw between ourselves as the observer, and all that is observed.

Humankind does make very productive use of our ability to distinguish, and label the separate parts of Ourself. The human mind's unique sophistication in this department is responsible for the enormous advances we have made in technology, as well as for the complexity of our social existence, and the vastness of our cultural achievements. This same capacity for segregating and labeling the different parts of Ourself is of course also, sadly, responsible for the incredible horrors of humanity's historical and present-day violence against itself, and the rest of the natural world.

Recognizing ourselves as part of one whole does not require us to repress or deny our ability to distinguish, but rather calls upon us to look beyond the horizon-line of our distinctions to the point where all things merge. We obviously rely on our powers of distinction to function in the world. Being aware of Ourself doesn't blur distinctions, but instead clarifies them because things can be understood more completely within a whole context. For example, if a zoologist wants to understand the unique traits of a species, she has to look at the total ecosystem it lives in. Viewing parts within the context of the whole illuminates the distinct traits of the parts.

This book is not about pretending that differences don't exist; it is about being aware equally of difference and commonality, and not letting difference blind us to our shared ultimate identity. Like the preceding hand/fingers analogy, we *can* be fully aware of both the uniqueness of the individual parts, and the magnificence of the whole. The transformation that occurs when we become conscious that our true identity is reality itself is not that we lose ourselves, but that we gain our whole self through our awareness that we are everything.

Reflection 1

Take a deep breath; drawing the air down as if from your feet. As you feel the airflow change directions between inhalation and exhalation, let every muscle in your body release all tension and control. Continue breathing slowly and deeply, and allow yourself to release any sounds that seem to want to come out as you exhale—moans, ahh's, mmm's, cries, or giggles. Calmly close your eyes, and listen to the sound of your breathing, while simultaneously listening to the inner sound of your thinking and feelings, and the sounds of the world around you. Try to locate the boundary between yourself and everything else around you. Similarly, try to locate the boundary between your outer self and your inner self. Where are these boundaries really? What are they composed of? Can you see that these boundaries do not actually exist—that they are composed of nothing, and are merely concepts or psychological assumptions? There is no exact location of the imaginary delineation between yourself and everything else, or between your inside and your outside. The sounds from inside and outside yourself are all the sounds of the single one thing that is everything happening at once; this "everything happening at once" is your most fundamental identity, or true nature. Continue to relax, breathing deeply, listening, and feeling your wholeness as Ourself being aware of Ourself.

Exploring, questioning, feeling, listening, and looking at *all* that we are within the wholeness of Ourself allows new insights and sensations to continually surface within us as we go about our busy and complex lives. We don't need to separate ourselves from the world by meditating in some lonely place, or hiding away in a monastery to awaken to the depths and wonders of our true nature. We simply need to engage fully with the world as Ourself.

This is not to deny the importance of quiet, rest, or solitude when we are moved to seek these, but instead to illuminate the truth that Ourself is everything, everywhere, all the time—during the quietest moments as well as during the loudest moments; during the most personal moments as well as the most social moments. If we could relate to each other primarily as Ourself, and secondarily as distinct individuals, then the reigning of the resultant respect and compassion would usher the world into a true state of peace.

When we are first introduced to the idea that we are actually one with everything everywhere, it can seem stifling if we react with fear and defensiveness—trying to protect our individual self-conception from being enveloped by the enormity of reality as a whole like some sort of alien force flooding us. However, when we let go of our fear and relax into purely witnessing ourselves and reality as a whole, then we can begin to understand that Ourself is not something alien or outside of ourselves that is taking us over, but is instead simply what we already are. All that we have ever been is Ourself manifesting the uniqueness that is us.

So there is no need to panic or feel threatened as if we are being overtaken by something external, because exactly the opposite is true. We can instead rejoice in opening ourselves completely to this profound awareness of what we have actually always been. Rather than being oppressed by oneness, we receive in being aware of ourselves as Ourself the freedom to spread our wings more fully than we ever have before.

If you don't like the name "Ourself," then freely create your own name for the one thing that everything actually is, but *don't* go on pretending that we are not actually all one thing interacting with itself. Why pretend? In pretending that we are all separate we feel a constant compulsion to define ourselves through materialism, professionalism, or eccentric-ism. Yet in spite of these efforts to increase the appearance that we are distinct and different, we paradoxically find ourselves simultaneously trying to "fit in" through conformity in a desperate attempt to maintain at least a superficial sense of connectedness with others, because deep down our core feelings tell us that we are not to be isolated from others.

By allowing ourselves to be aware of our true, holistic identity, Ourself, we can naturally be aware of both our uniqueness and our commonality. We can then consciously take pleasure in manifesting our unique talents and qualities throughout our lives, while also experiencing a true sense of communion and understanding with others. Actually experiencing ourselves as the oneness that is *everything* and *everyone* is the first step towards, "getting a life." In discovering that our primary identity is the shared wholeness of Ourself we become free to wander fully and securely into our secondary identity as unique individuals.

This book is not a book of philosophy, religion, or science; it is a book of utter simplicity. In essence it provides a word to use in reference to that which includes all other words, ideas, truths, objects, entities, and realities within itself. The author sincerely hopes that the word *Ourself* will set in motion an ongoing process of adjustment by humankind to the fact that we are all first and foremost one thing interacting with Ourself. We should be striving to develop appropriate ways of interacting with each other and the natural environment as parts of Ourself instead of as separate entities using, abusing, and destroying each other as we are doing in the world at present. Though we may constantly forget that we are Ourself, and we may be constantly encouraged to forget this by a world that emphasizes separateness, we can always return to our awareness of Ourself instantaneously by simply allowing our awareness to gently embrace the struggle, stress, guilt, and doubt of our thinking while recognizing that every thought, feeling, and perspective is merely a different mask of Ourself.

Rather than focusing on trying to see beyond our thinking to find Ourself, we instead need to look right *into* our thinking, and see that it too is just Ourself. Our thinking is Ourself doing a convincing job of telling itself a narrative which denies that Ourself exists, and that instead reality is a bunch of disconnected parts, and that we as individual human beings are inherently separate from everything and everyone else. The trick is not to stop thinking, but to stop being so faithfully duped by the individualistic tone in our thinking. Our thinking is amazingly deceitful in that it mesmerizes us with the individualistic tone of every thought into believing unquestionably in our separateness.

We are so used to constantly thinking in separate individual-istic terms that even when our mind is at rest the powerful sensation of separateness lingers so that the instant we begin thinking or talking, we pick up right where we left off in our fragmenting narrative. Merely experiencing quiet within ourselves is not enough, we need to actually see and recognize that our thoughts themselves are Ourself; the very sensation of separateness our minds produce *is* Ourself. We must look fully into every separate-toned thought, and see that our whole experience as a separate entity is actually Ourself thinking to, and experiencing, itself.

We mustn't be timid about this as it is a matter of great urgency. Only in becoming aware of our true identity, Ourself, can we manifest our lives to the fullest in accordance with our unique roles within the whole. To try to "get a life," or "be yourself," while stuck in the isolating illusion of separateness is like attempting to lift your body off of the ground by pulling on your own shoelaces; it's not really possible because "your" self as a *separate entity* doesn't actually exist. Such glorified concepts as "self-actualization" or "self fulfillment" seem petty and minute when compared to the much deeper and broader process of receiving change and growth through the inner lift of discovering the absolute wholeness of Ourself.

Ourself is more than a "new age" or Eastern concept such as

"nothingness," "formlessness," or "mindfulness"—it is *alive*! Ourself is the eternal, raw, primordial living essence of reality that we are all made of. Ourself's depth, love, and power are unfathomable, and infinitely beautiful and sublime. Ourself is the one real thing that everything is merely a facet of, and as a whole its immensity and intensity of feeling extend unimaginably far beyond our ability to consider or perceive. Getting to know the all encompassing soul of Ourself is even better than meeting the best "soul mate" or friend you could ever dream of, or wish for. Ourself is everything, and in that "everything" we can find all the inspiration and understanding that we seek. Once we have met Ourself, we no longer rely on others to confirm our insights or guidance because we have met the real teacher of everyone, that *is* in fact everyone—Ourself.

Chapter 2

Being Ourself

What does it mean to *be* Ourself? If Ourself is everything, then isn't everyone always *being* Ourself? Yes, but that's just it—how often are we really aware of this throughout the day, the year, our entire lives? How often do we deeply feel at home with *everything* and *everybody* as Ourself? Ultimately we don't have any choice in being Ourself because that is simply what we are, but we can choose to consciously explore what we are with greater integrity; not with our analytical thinking but with pure, curious awareness.

If we can stop engaging in our thinking for once, and just observe it without judging or interfering, and really allow ourselves to feel where it comes from, where the movement of each thought begins, we will find that the elaborate performances of thought all move forth within us from the same anonymous silence and stillness that we can observe by looking at our body externally. Take a minute to look at your body and recognize its silence and stillness. Now look around you at your surroundings, and recognize that same silence and stillness in everything. As you think any thoughts that come about, glimpse that they move forth from that same silence and stillness. All movement comes out of this silence and stillness, whether it is in the realm of our thinking, or whether it is the sudden jump of a silent and still rabbit suddenly startled.

Being Ourself for real means allowing our side blinders to be removed by this silent, penetrating, ever present brilliance of naked reality that eternally glows within us and all around us so that we can really recognize and comprehend the holistic scenario we are all part of. We are truly *reality witnessing reality*. We are both the stillness and the motion of reality interacting with itself. Being Ourself means living our lives with this one-thing-vision.

One-thing-vision involves constantly looking and feeling beyond the superficial appearance of separateness, and reaching for the subtle, deep pulse of Ourself in every moment. There is an essential quality or look that all things share in common that we need to become aware of both in ourselves and in all that surrounds us—the one-thing-look. This silent presence sings out from everything, but it takes patience to become conscious of. It's like when you walk into a dimly lit room from outside on a sunny day; your eyes have to adjust to the change in light before they can see.

As you search for Ourself, you have to let your consciousness adjust to the light of Ourself's silent presence within your thoughts and consciousness, and simultaneously within your body and surroundings. You might need to take a deep breath and slow down to let the one-thing-look emerge from the blur of busyness and self-preoccupation that so effectively hide reality's true face. You are allowing reality's wholeness to come into view by seeing, hearing, and feeling the one essential quality that *everything* shares in common.

As you look, listen, and feel for Ourself you have to realize that you are not looking for anything other than what you already see and already are. We won't find Ourself by trying to see something strange or unusual. Ourself is not unusual; it's just unusual for people to notice Ourself subtly glowing within everything. In truth, Ourself is the most ordinary thing there is—it's just reality.

If we have thought reality mundane, we might need to stare down the mundane exterior we have psychologically draped over reality in the process of reducing it to a bunch of disconnected and identified parts. If you really probe into the mundane, you will find the miracle of existence, Ourself, within it. When you have seen through the humdrum façade of everything portrayed by thought as a massive collection of separate parts which *do not* share a common source and substance, and have recognized the brilliant mysteriousness of creation which all of these apparently separate parts are dripping with, then you will no longer be trapped in a dreary perspective of reality. If we really want to experience our lives within this majestic wholeness—if we want to consciously be Ourself—we need to thoroughly and directly see, hear, feel, smell, touch, and taste reality first-hand, both within us and all around us.

Ourself might be easier to recognize in quiet and tranquil natural settings, but this silent presence exists even in the noisiest and most horrific places. By being deeply committed to looking, listening, and feeling for Ourself in every moment of our lives, we become aware that Ourself's wisdom, guidance, and solace are always abundantly available to us. If we are accustomed to staying in touch with our true identity, Ourself, throughout the day, then we will have an easier time finding Ourself's guidance and solace during urgent times of need.

For it is during difficult and stressful times—when we need Ourself's solace and guidance the most—that it can be most difficult to see beyond the appearance of separateness and self-isolation; because in our desperation we think and feel more acutely which further emphasizes the sensation of "me, myself, and I" as an isolated and separate identity. This is the value of making a deep, lifelong commitment, like a marriage vow, to being Ourself. As in a marriage, the more committed we are to being Ourself, the more enduringly profound, comforting, and ecstatic our experience of life as Ourself will be.

When we recognize the one-thing-look of Ourself within ourselves and everything else the real juices of life begin to flow; filling our lives with that wondrous, vibrant, and open inner-atmosphere which we all ultimately crave and need. This immense energy, which surfaces within us whenever we recognize that we are actually all one thing, Ourself, is the steam we need to get us through the constant challenges and pains which life brims over with.

This is not to say that we can always be happy—the full spectrum of human emotions is natural and healthy—but as long as we are aware of ourselves as Ourself, our sails will be full of the subtle grace of Ourself which provides the inner stability we need to move through the murky, deep waters of emotion which human beings must feel to be whole and fully alive. The inner propulsion and lubrication required to keep our feelings from getting stuck can only enduringly be found through the holistic perspective of ourselves and reality as Ourself. They say that "time heals," but what that really means is that *reality heals* eventually. The more we are able to open our closed conception of personal ownership of our problems and pains, and to let reality's light in by allowing ourselves to experience difficult situations and emotions as Ourself experiencing Ourself, the faster the healing presence of reality's light can do its work.

What primarily gets in the way of us being Ourself is our mind's preoccupation with thinking about ourselves as separate. Once a lie has been told, you either need to continue telling more lies to support the original lie, or else surrender and admit the truth. This is a scary process to our minds, and most of us don't even realize that we have told ourselves a lie—the lie that we are inherently separate individuals. We are so caught up in continuing with every thought the fictional storyline of ourselves as separate, that we completely fail to notice that this entire lifelong monologue is merely Ourself thinking to itself.

Even our bodies which appear to clearly be physically independent from our surroundings are not actually in any way separate from the rest of physical reality; as even the most elementary understanding of physics reveals to us. Our physical body is merely part of the endless flow of matter which composes the universe. The reality-stuff we eat, drink and breathe literally becomes our body, and then continues on its way as our breath, sweat, and wastes.

Our mind's constant preoccupation with our individual identity, needs, and desires in the form of the endless monologue in our consciousness revolving around "I" or "me," completely robs us of our true identity, Ourself. The only way to become aware of this true identity is to recognize the one-thing-look of Ourself right smack dab in the middle of every thought and feeling we experience so that we discontinue being fooled into perceiving ourselves and our thoughts as existing somehow apart from the rest of reality. Obviously this kind of seeing is not merely the kind of seeing we can do with our eyes alone. One-thing-vision requires us to be aware of our entire consciousness as the essence of reality being aware of itself.

When we witness our own thinking as part of Ourself, the presumption of separateness which underlies our thoughts no longer seems so concrete. As we grow in awareness and maturity we hopefully come to see this sensation of separateness for what it really is—just a sensation. Without trying to kill or resist the sensation of "I" or "me," we need to relax and allow ourselves to be aware of our sensation of "I" or "me" simultaneously with the sights and sounds of reality around us. Rather than identifying with our thoughts as being our "selves," we have to hear and feel our thoughts and emotions as part of the whole sound and movement of Ourself.

Our thoughts, feelings, and bodies are merely aspects of one whole which goes on infinitely both inwardly and outwardly. No separate essence is somehow stuck inside of our thoughts or our body. No little glowing ball exists in the center of each individual person with our name on it forming anything that could legitimately be considered separate from the rest of reality. Just the way our body is merely part of the continuum of the physical aspect of Ourself, our spiritual self is just part of the continuum of the inner aspect of Ourself. Allowing the illusions of an icy core and an icy exoskeleton to be melted away by the primordial warmth of Ourself is what being Ourself is all about. We need to let the all-pervasive truth and wonder of Ourself uncap our bottled up feeling of separateness forever.

This locked in feeling of "me-ness" which most of us carry around—which we usually identify with our name, our thoughts, our preferences, and our bodies—is nothing more than a feeling or sensation which is the product of thought. Our thinking manufactures and maintains this multidimensional illusion of separateness through a combination of memory, imagery, and vocabulary which all stem from the incomplete perception of our bodies as being separate from the rest of physical reality. Unfortunately, we mistakenly assume that because our bodies appear separate—and we have a plethora of memories, images, and words which all support this appearance of separateness—we must therefore actually be separate. Similarly we mistakenly assume that because we can label and identify different aspects or parts of reality as separate, that all these aspects of reality which we label and identify separately must actually be separate.

This mistaken assumption of separateness snowballs throughout our lives as we continue to pile a never-ending heap of memories and impressions within our thoughts and feelings which continuously add weight to the sensation of separateness. The process of being Ourself involves displacing this heavy sensation of separateness through recognizing the cognitive error we have made throughout our lives in perceiving everything as fundamentally separate. Our ever-growing awareness of ourselves as Ourself reveals to us that the illusion of separateness is an inevitable by-product of the mechanics of human thought.

In every moment we each face a profound opportunity to transcend the facade of separateness by looking with deep vigilance at the processes within our mind, and recognizing the one-thing-look of Ourself simultaneously throughout these internal processes and throughout the world around us. In other words, when we finally distinguish that everything "outside" of us has the same essential identity as everything "inside" of us, we will then experience the true absolution of Ourself.

Often we think of our face as a reliable or permanent part of our self-identity, but if you look closely at a collection of photographs of yourself you will see that there is no absolute "you" to be found in your face either. You might like the person you see in some photos, and be embarrassed by the person you see in others. Our face, body, feelings, and thoughts are all constantly changing. If, however, we can start to look for the face of Ourself concurrently within ourselves and in all that surrounds us, we will find that this face is the everlasting face—our universally true face as indivisible aspects of reality—and that this face is to be seen everywhere when we look with the penetrating integrity of Ourself.

As a window to observing this face of Ourself, look at each of your fingers as an entity. View your fingernails as your fingers' faces—they stair back at you silently. I used to do this as a child; I thought they looked like little nuns—the fingernail as the face, and the fleshy part around the nail as the wimple, or head-cloth that nuns used to wear. Can you see the one-thing-look of Ourself staring back at you from your little nun-like fingernail faces? Now look around you, and recognize that same silent face staring back at you from everything. This is the face of Ourself.

My earliest memory of seeing this silent face staring back at me is as a toddler looking at the bright green peas on my plate. Each pea seemed to be looking at me with the same silent face. I don't know why people say, "You can't see God." The silent face of reality, the one-thing-look of Ourself, *is* God's face; we can see it *everywhere* because everything is Ourself. In other words, reality's source (referred to by some as "God"), is ever-present throughout reality's substance (referred to by some as "creation"); the whole of source and substance is Ourself.

How does this one-thing-look of Ourself become so unfamiliar to most of us? Our thinking minds and our feeling hearts, both of which promote an isolated sense of self, never stop moving or distracting us from the one-thing-look, and eventually we forget all about Ourself. Based on this, some people have put forth the misleading notion that peace or enlightenment is a state where your mind or feelings stop, but that's not really enlightenment— that's death. Sometimes we find our mind quiet and calm, but some degree of psychological motion always exists if you are really alive.

Developing the ability to stop ourselves from thinking has nothing to do with freedom from the self; in fact it only strengthens the self. The deadening process of self-repression can only further a person from becoming familiar with what is natural and real, Ourself. A mind which can "shut up" is not a quiet mind, just a tense and obedient one. A child who remains quiet, or behaves according to certain standards because of fear of reprimand doesn't exhibit purity; purity exists when a child feels truly free to feel and express what is authentic. Peace and enlightenment aren't about self-control or mind control; they are about profound acceptance of your thoughts and feelings born through consciousness of your thoughts and feelings as Ourself.

Rather than trying to make your mind "shut up," simply let the one-thing-vision of all that is going on around and within you to displace your mind from center stage. In other words, let the attention being given to your body and your surroundings come into balance with the attention being given to your thoughts and feelings. As you experience the realization that everything going on both inside and around you is all part of one total movement, you will discover the enormous feeling of simplicity and freedom which come about through this awareness.

When a slide projector image of a single object is out of focus the image appears to be of two objects. As you adjust the projector's focus dial the two objects move together until you can finally distinguish that there is only one object. This process parallels what happens within ourselves as we come into focus with Ourself. We ordinarily perceive our minds and bodies as separate from the rest of reality, but when we relax and allow our consciousness to come into focus with reality as a whole we are suddenly able to distinguish that *we are* reality. There are not two things—ourselves as opposed to the rest of reality. There is only *one* thing that is everything and everyone, everywhere—Ourself.

Just as a slide projector needs to be brought back into focus by the hand of something beyond it (a human hand adjusting the dial), we need to be brought back into focus with reality through the hand of something beyond ourselves. The more we try to see ourselves as one with everything from the perspective of our own thinking, the more we accentuate our apparent separateness. The tension created by the obvious contradiction of a self trying not to be a self distances us further from the natural awareness of ourselves as Ourself.

This phenomenon is reminiscent of a Chinese finger-trap—a finger-wide, woven, tube shaped toy that you stick your fingers into the ends of. Once you have placed your fingers into either end, the harder you try to pull your fingers out, the more the trap's woven grip tightens and holds your fingers. We need to stop trying from within the perspective of ourselves as something separate—from "me, myself, and I"—to see that we are in fact not separate. The wholeness of Ourself is so simple and straight-forward that we have a hard time recognizing it; like the saying, "It's right under your nose." It is only through letting go of our self-centered effort to be free from our "self" that we are released into the liberating wholeness of Ourself.

Nonetheless, once you have seen the one-thing-look of Ourself clearly you will still find that like high and low tide at the beach, our awareness of ourselves as Ourself comes and goes. This is the ongoing spiritual work of life—living with the constant intention of recognizing that everything is Ourself. It requires perpetual abandonment of the temptation to be captivated by our thoughts' and feelings' portrayal of everything as separate. We have to leave a window open in our consciousness at all times to allow the fresh air of Ourself to move and circulate within our thoughts and feelings, so that they don't gather the misleading momentum of the appearance of separateness.

The light of Ourself frames our awareness of our thoughts and feelings within reality as a whole, leaving us with a peace and confidence which can only come about through the recognition that what is outside is of the same essential nature as what is inside. In the process, the busy monologue of "I" is bumped from center stage and instead becomes merely one voice in the vast audience of everyone and everything, which is Ourself.

It is comparable to an orchestra—if the brass section or the percussion section is playing too loudly, then it drowns out the more subtle voices of the wind and string instruments, and leaves the musical composition as a whole barely recognizable. When our thoughts and feelings have total domination of our consciousness and maintain the absolute sensation of inherent isolation which most of us live our lives out with, we lose the truthful and sane perspective of Ourself. We can no longer recognize the actual song of Ourself because we are only hearing one small part of the whole.

If we can relax and be aware of ourselves as part of everything, then we can become aware of ourselves as useful and meaningful instruments of Ourself. By outgrowing the sensation of ownership which we feel about our thoughts and bodies, and realizing that everything we are is only part of something bigger, we can come to understand our unique roles within Ourself just as we understand the unique roles of our various organs—such as the heart, lungs, and brain—within our body as a whole.

As you become less obstructed by the sensation of yourself as separate, you will discover a new clarity as part of Ourself about which directions to move in life. This is what the word guidance is about—feeling movement and direction within ourselves, informed by and originating from deep within Ourself, allowing us to move and act in harmony with the whole of Ourself.

This is comparable to the way our legs are informed by our brains how to work together to enable us to walk. If our legs were only conscious of themselves as separate body parts consumed with their own thoughts and feelings, and only moved to their own self-centered impulses, then it would be pretty hard for our brains to get our legs to perform together enabling us to walk. When we are similarly cut off from Ourself by constant preoccupation with our own thoughts and feelings we find ourselves not only overcome with an incredibly painful sense of isolation and emptiness, but also unable to harmoniously flow with the people and events of our lives.

Being Ourself consists of going beyond the limits of self-awareness, and allowing ourselves to be moved and guided by Ourself from moment to moment in our daily lives. It involves more than what some people refer to as "mindfulness." Really being Ourself involves a totally willing engagement with the ecstatic freedom and immensity of the one living being that we are all facets of, and allowing ourselves to be genuinely moved and guided from this freedom and immensity. Becoming fluid in this way allows us to better serve the broader needs of Ourself— including the needs of both humanity and the environment—and it similarly allows us to better serve our individual needs because Ourself understands the complex nuances of our deepest needs, and how they symbiotically fit with the needs of others, in ways that the "me, myself, and I" of our conscious minds can not.

As we open ourselves up to the guidance of Ourself, we find our needs being fulfilled in richer, more meaningful ways than we have ever dreamed of. When we live with one-thing-vision it is as though Ourself begins to develop our lives from inside and outside simultaneously. In other words, as we lose the sensation that everything "outside" of us is separate we begin to increasingly experience the emergence of a surprisingly complementary relationship between what we had previously thought of dichotomously as "me" versus "everything else." The word "grace" originates from this surprising ability of Ourself to shift and shape both inwardly and outwardly simultaneously; the result of which is a feeling of serendipity, awe, and gratitude as we find our consciousness serving as a permeable link between the inner and outer dimensions of Ourself.

The longer we live our lives with the one-thing-vision Ourself, the more we notice a harmony developing between our needs, and the needs of those around us. Ourself can arrange mutually advantageous relationships and situations much more richly and readily than our isolated plotting minds. Ourself enabled humans to conceive of clocks with their interlocking, and interdependent gears, and Ourself conceives of much grander and more beautifully complex interlocking parts than those of clocks. There are amazing relationships between the different parts of Ourself, as any biologist can tell you using examples from the amazing symbiotic relationships that exist in the plant and animal kingdoms. As we become more aware of life as Ourself we begin acutely noticing these relationships, correlations, and story lines that develop between people, places, trees, animals, colors, songs, events, and all the other aspects of life.

At first being aware of yourself as Ourself may seem like an unusual experience, but as you go on you will realize that what many people consider to be some kind of mystical state is actually completely natural; it's just a matter of being what we are—Ourself. Humans tend to portray ultimate truth, reality, or God—which are all synonyms for Ourself—as being out of reach and impossible to see, but all of these words simply refer to the one thing that everything is all the time.

We alienate ourselves from Ourself in this way to evade responsibility for seeing the big picture in every moment of our lives, and to shield ourselves from the often demanding implications of seeing the holistic reality of Ourself. Ourself is a starkly complex collective of interwoven phenomena that includes all of us. To live up to our roles within this interdependent life requires a great deal of effort and exertion from everyone to keep humanity's and the earth's needs taken care of. By keeping the true perspective of Ourself out of focus, we create an opportunity for ourselves to not live up to the magnificent ways of Ourself, and then we indulge in doubt and guilt as ways of further escaping having to face Ourself.

When a whole culture is committed to blinding itself to the fundamental truth of the great oneness, and promotes the myth that the creator is distant and impossible for ordinary people to commune with, it succeeds in dividing people psychologically, and in cutting them off from their true identity and source of spiritual inspiration and sustenance, Ourself. The effect of such a subtle and prolonged form of mass hysteria is that it squanders the intelligence and the integrity of the culture. Nonetheless, certain individuals within such cultures continue to be haunted by life's profound questions such as, "Who am I?" and, "What is reality?"

To avoid having to look at these difficult questions, and the answer to them, Ourself, most people either busy themselves with the superficial details of daily life—pretending that life is not inherently profound and spiritual—or instead cling to rigid and dogmatic interpretations of life, ranging from atheism to religious fundamentalism, which are really two sides of the same coin. Humans apparently find it more tempting to avoid the one-thing-look of Ourself which is lurking everywhere at all times—by continuously participating in the ridiculous work of maintaining a separate identity through constantly engaging with our thinking seriously and literally—than to instead jump right into the divine, three dimensional vividness of Ourself. By all of us collectively avoiding the one-thing-vision of Ourself together, we effectively avoid almost any chance of consciously being Ourself.

Fortunately there is something powerful that dwells within many people that is allergic to falseness, and causes them to challenge the assumptions of their given cultural milieu. Any hope for humanity to find lasting peace and happiness rests on the shoulders of such people. They have the courage to see what really is. When they eventually challenge the most fundamental assumption of the mind—separateness—they recognize the one-thing-look of Ourself staring out from everything inside and outside all at once. If we could all follow in their footsteps, and outgrow our fear and resistance to being Ourself, we could quickly and radically transform this world into a brighter, more loving, healthier and happier world.

Being Ourself shouldn't be a one-time event, or an isolated "spiritual experience." Being Ourself is an ongoing process of constantly looking for the one-thing-look of Ourself within every thought, feeling, and circumstance that threatens to throw us off Ourself's scent. Through our awareness that we are Ourself in every moment we can see through the distracting diversions of guilt, shame, and doubt which our minds so often cling to as ways of maintaining the facades of self-atonement and self-improvement. In reality guilt, shame and doubt are merely threads of the illusive web of separate identity that our minds are constantly spinning.

The inconsistency between the conception of ourselves as implicitly separate creatures and the reality that we are actually mere aspects of Ourself leaves us with the sense deep down that something is not quite right. This is the real source of humanity's fundamental angst, alienation, and anxiety spoken of by the existentialist philosophers. Instead of simply facing the simple fact that we are principally Ourself, and recognizing our true place within the wholeness of existence, we instead associate this "not quite right" feeling with whatever qualities of ours we are insecure, ashamed, or embarrassed by in order to support our mind's charade of innate separateness. In other words, we say to ourselves unconsciously, "The reason I don't feel quite right is because I am imperfect and I should therefore work towards perfecting myself, and then I will feel better." This helps us to feel as though we have acknowledged the source of our uneasy feeling, and simultaneously reinforces our sense of separateness by framing the uneasy feeling in the context of the self as a separate entity merely in need of a few improvements.

Really becoming comfortable in our own skin results from developing a revolutionary kind of self-honesty as Ourself. What lies behind humanity's dis-ease is the fact that our entire psychological identity is built upon the false premise that we are each inherently separate entities. In becoming conscious that we are all solely Ourself, we begin to step out of our compulsive addiction to the distractions of guilt, shame, and doubt, and similarly their opposites—pride and arrogance. By consciously being Ourself we become familiar with a profound new kind of self-acceptance through the natural and sustaining confidence and humility of Ourself. Every moment of our lives is a moment in the company of everything else—guilt, shame, doubt, pride, and arrogance are all melded by the blaze of Ourself.

Reflection 2

Sit or stand comfortably, and inhale slowly deep into your belly and lower back. Exhale, and let go of all focus or obsession within yourself. Look around you, and at your own body, slowly moving your head and vision without stopping on any one object. Allow yourself to see through color and shape, recognizing the one essential quality shared by everything. Like a clay-mation movie where all the objects and characters are all actually clay in different colors and shapes, see that everything is actually the reality-stuff of Ourself in different colors and shapes. See, hear, and feel everything inside you and around you as reality interacting with itself, thinking to itself, and being aware of itself. As you breathe deeply, continue to be conscious of everything as one whole in the same way that you perceive all the different parts of your body as one whole body. Be aware of all of existence, including all that you are, as Ourself's single, all encompassing, eternal body of change. Let the subtle but ever-present intelligence of Ourself express itself in your consciousness. Feel the eternal dance of source and substance that is you; that is all that surrounds you; that is everything up, and everything down; everything to the left, and everything to the right. Recognize Ourself as your thoughts; recognize Ourself as your body; recognize Ourself as the Earth; and feel Ourself extending upwards right through the sky into the infinite. This is being Ourself...

As you become familiar with feeling and seeing yourself and everything else as Ourself, begin to explore what it feels like to carry this awareness into your daily life. As you crack an egg into a frying pan, and flip the egg as it cooks, be aware of the egg, the frying pan, the spatula, the floor, the stove, the sizzle, and yourself, all as Ourself. The next time you go for a drive be conscious of your thoughts, your feelings, your breathing, your hands, the steering wheel, the car, the wheels, the road, the other cars, the people walking down the sidewalk, the houses and trees, all as the one phenomenon Ourself. The next time you go for a walk, brush your teeth, or engage in any other activity, enjoy the BIG feeling of being Ourself in action.

Being Ourself—consciously living our lives with one-thing-vision—has a very real sense of magic or the miraculous about it. The ordinary appears extra-ordinary when you tune in to the fundamental quality of Ourself that exists within everything. Do you remember the first time you rode a bike without training wheels, and were really able to do it? That grand sense of freedom and exhilaration doesn't need to be a lost moment from childhood—when you are being Ourself, any activity you do takes on that amazing feeling. It is a fundamental sense of awe over the fact that we can move about in these incredible bodies which are like moving sculptures that can see the world, hear music, taste food, and smell beauty. The fundamental miraculousness of existence comes to light when you recognize the one-thing-look in everything—when you discover the one-thing-vision of Ourself, for yourself.

When you no longer feel first and foremost like "me, Jane Doe," or "me, John Doe," but instead begin to feel like "everything, Ourself," the inner light bulb clicks on and everything makes a little more sense than it did before. This is not to say that you will suddenly feel ambivalent towards the horror and tragedy that exist in the world, but that within the silent presence of Ourself you will receive a subtle yet crucial solace. Pain will still hurt, pleasure will still feel good, but there will be a balancing element within all experience—the eternal presence of Ourself staring at you from everywhere inside and out all at once.

As you develop some consistency in your awareness that you are Ourself, then your individual experience as "me, John Doe," or "me, Jane Doe," will also begin to feel very different. Your awareness of your individual identity will no longer be so narrow, frantic, petulant, or heavy. Your individual name, body, and characteristics will seem like an identity to work with, not a permanent fixture. You will become aware of your many gifts and talents, and how to use them as parts of Ourself. Like a painting where every individual stroke combines to make a beautiful whole, a world full of people developing their uniqueness and abilities within the united framework of Ourself would make a similarly beautiful whole. Can't we all see the sense in this? Isn't it clear that this world can be a more harmonious, bountiful, and glorious place if we allow ourselves to be more aware of the common identity we all share as aspects of the same one thing, Ourself?

Chapter 3

Finding Ourselves in Ourself

It might seem that we would lose our sense of unique individual character in the process of realizing that no actual separation exists between ourselves and the rest of reality. However, it is actually through seeing ourselves within the holistic scenario of everything that we are fully able to perceive our unique qualities and talents as distinct parts of Ourself. Recognizing ourselves as Ourself, we finally glimpse the "real me," reality as a whole, and the myriad ways we fit into the vast ensemble of Ourself become illuminated.

If you remove one word from a great poem, or one thread from a beautiful tapestry, and study the word or thread in isolation, then you can no longer see the significance or role of that one word or thread. However, placed within the poem or tapestry, the word or thread's true pattern and purpose can be wholly seen and understood in context. Similarly, we need to develop our ability to see ourselves within the tapestry of Ourself in order to understand our unique roles and patterns within the broader patterns of the whole.

Finding yourself in Ourself is "being Ourself" in action. If you only familiarize yourself with wholeness in stillness and quiet, then you won't be able to recognize or participate in the great dance of Ourself. While we can get a taste of the authentic motion of Ourself while watching others perform, we can only fully experience the magnitude of this living freedom through our own receiving of action and movement.

It is as though our bodies are a glove that when we were born had the vibrant hand of Ourself moving within it, but as we psychologically developed the static sensation of innate separateness, the glove began to close up and become rigid, so that the hand of Ourself could no longer move the glove freely. Eventually the hand of Ourself could no longer fit into the stiffened glove, and the opening of the glove closed up. We were so busy living our daily lives that we failed to notice this gradual, disastrous change within us. At some point, however, we many of us start to notice the emptiness and pain of being cut off from the movement and pulse of Ourself, and we begin to wonder what we are missing. We begin to wonder, "Why do I feel so separate, isolated, and shut down inside?"

As our pain and alienation reach a peak, we become penetratingly aware of the falseness of this sense of separation, and the stifled or lifeless quality of what has become like a rigidified glove. It is through this critical yet sincere inner crescendo that the entrance to the glove is re-opened. As we begin to remember and recognize our fundamental and collective identity, Ourself, the hand of Ourself begins to creep back into the glove and move us freely again. For the glove to become fully supple we need to give Ourself ample opportunity to regularly and thoroughly rouse us.

This is the value of the wide array of activities humans engage in—to allow us to dynamically experience the movement and guidance of Ourself in our daily lives. When we find activities that profoundly resonate with our unique gifts and talents, and begin practicing and developing these activities, we find ourselves becoming increasingly pliable as our awareness of Ourself deepens and expands through this movement. We are not meant to solely be spectators—we are the doers: the inventors, the actors, the caretakers, the artists, the nurturers, the musicians, the organizers, and the lovers.

Because there are endless ways in which we can participate with and contribute to Ourself, it can be hard to know where to jump in. In order to discover the unique, primordial patterns within ourselves which most boldly emanate the magic and wonder of Ourself, we all must pay careful attention to which activities in life ignite our deepest enthusiasm. If we have begun to lose track of what activities we really have zest for, then uncovering these essential patterns of our being may require us to shed many layers of imitative characteristics, concerns, and behaviors which have accumulated throughout our lifetime. We need to have intense self-honesty to initiate this process. By coming to understand ourselves within the true perspective of Ourself we can eventually be freed from the influences which have covered up and perhaps disabled our vital qualities.

For most of us the discovery of which spokes we are in the wheel of Ourself is gradual and multifaceted. For example, many people don't have a single outstanding talent or characteristic upon which they will base their life. Most of us are more like musical chords made up of multiple notes—the combination of all of our subtle and different characteristics, and interests, forms our unique place within Ourself. We need to remain open and willing as we move through our lives in order to become aware of the many contributions we each have to offer Ourself.

However, some of us may be taken with so many different activities that it becomes hard to sort out which we really want to focus on; not to mention the challenge of figuring out which activities we want to develop to support our lives materially. To begin finding ourselves in Ourself we need to consider which activities we find most meaningful, and which activities seem to rob us of the time and energy required to really pursue these. Also we need to explore what resistances or hesitations we have towards pursuing activities that we really are interested in, but have either quit because of past failures, frustrations, and embarrassments, or have simply never pursued with real dedication. Ourself can help us sort all this out if we are truly open to letting it.

Initiating a dialogue with Ourself is the first step towards this end. As in any dialogue we must thoughtfully craft our questions, and listen openly to the answers. It is important to be aware that a dialogue with Ourself is really a conversation between one part of yourself and another, or between Ourself as a thinking brain and Ourself the infinite. Because the aspect of yourself that asks the questions (the thinking mind) is not the aspect of yourself that knows the answers (Ourself the infinite), the answers to the thinking mind's questions can not necessarily be understood in the thinking mind's terms.

In order to allow Ourself to answer your mind's pressing questions you need to accustom yourself to hearing and feeling the nonverbal language of Ourself. Interpreting guidance from Ourself is more like watching a mime performance than reading a telegram. Learning to feel and distinguish answers in this intuitive realm of Ourself is the most important ability we can develop as human beings because this is what allows us to sort through the absurdly wide array of possibilities and choices which life confronts us with. If we want to "get a life"—to discover what we are really here to do, and to start doing it—then we need to have access to Ourself's nonverbal wisdom and guidance.

Don't look to other people to help you figure out what you are really interested in; you need to receive this inspiration from within. Also, don't worry if you aren't receiving grand revelations about who you are, or what you should be doing. Lighten up your expectations about what it is like to receive guidance or inspiration from Ourself. It is often a subtle process of recognition that we may not even realize is happening. In fact we may not notice that an understanding has begun to grow in us about something we have been wondering about until after the fact.

When we try too hard to understand Ourself's guidance we block our ability to understand because we are thinking too much about it. If we can learn to patiently ask a question and let it sink into the depths of Ourself, then the answer will surface in its own time, and in its own way—often when we least expect it. Something somebody says, a scene in a movie, or a word on a billboard might be the trigger; you never know how Ourself will communicate to your conscious mind. The answer might just become clear to us out of nowhere as we step into the bath, "Eureka!"

We don't get to choose what Ourself reveals to us. Sometimes we aren't ready to consciously understand the answers to our questions. Sometimes it's a matter of timing—we might need to proceed in ignorance to accidentally discover an answer, or to allow circumstances to fall into place that will make the answer clear to us. Ultimately we can only try to make the most of whatever understanding we *are* given, and to show our gratitude by acting on our guidance.

As we begin looking at what activities we most enjoy, we might feel insecurities because some activities that interest us may not seem glamorous or important. However, an immeasurable array of activities must occur daily to keep humanity and the rest of Ourself thriving. If you truly recognize that as an inseparable part of Ourself you have intrinsic value and purpose, then Ourself will increasingly reveal what your unique value and purpose are. If you are really willing to work and to play, then Ourself will show you how. You'll know when you have found the kinds of activities that you are made to do, because when you get around other people doing them you will feel a powerful urge to join in; like when you hear a song that makes you want to stand up and start singing or dancing along.

We often think of desire as a "bad" thing. We assume that we must control our desires, or they will lead us into doing things we'll later regret. It's true that some desires do need to be controlled—not because these desires are "bad," but because they interfere with or sabotage more fundamental desires we have in our lives. The key is to regularly sort through your desires, and to figure out which ones are most important to you and have the greatest potential to deepen and enrich your experience of yourself as Ourself.

To find ourselves in Ourself we have to develop an intimate knowledge of our desires, and avoid getting stuck in resisting or belittling our desires. As we discover which desires are the most fundamental to our feeling good about ourselves, and which ones will distract us from achieving these fundamental desires, we begin to access our most obvious compass for navigating the activities of our lives.

After all, why do we have desires if not to guide us? Were we really made full of desires so that we could spend our whole lives repressing them in misery? Beliefs like that are condescending to the ultimate intelligence of Ourself, nature, God, evolution, or whatever other word you want to use to indicate the creative source of humanity's existence. The problem for many of us is that we don't take the time to sincerely and seriously sort through our web of desires before acting. We don't prioritize our desires so as to ensure that we won't trip ourselves up by impulsively following our every little whim.

If we fully explore the various desires within ourselves we find that our most fundamental desires are not selfish in an exclusionary way, but instead are selfish in the sense of being in the best interests of our ultimate self or identity, Ourself. These higher-desires become evident as we begin routinely sorting through our desires, seeing them completely without repressing or editing them, and then recognizing which desires have real priority in our lives. This is the ongoing process of finding ourselves in the light of Ourself.

Reflection 3

Get a pen and paper and start freely writing down your desires. Think of as many as you can without editing them, or judging them as excessive, selfish, or wrong. This is a chance to become intimately acquainted with your desires, and you can not do that if you are not completely honest with yourself.

When you have truly exhausted your well of desires, read through your list and circle the ones which if not realized will never allow you to truly feel complete about your life. Now go through the desires you have circled, and pick the top three to write down on a fresh piece of paper; leaving a little bit of space to write between each one.

Look at the first desire on your top three list, and make a list under it of all the different people who would benefit from this desire being realized. Next to this list make a list of any people this desire would actually harm if realized. Do the same with the other two desires from your top three list.

Now eliminate any of your top three desires that would harm somebody, and replace them with other desires from your full list. Again list any people who would be harmed, and any people who would benefit from these desires being realized. Continue this process until you have narrowed your top three list down to three desires which would not harm anybody.

When you have finished picking three desires that would not harm anybody else then you have successfully identified at least three of your most fundamental desires. As you enter every day you can now focus on what it will take to realize these desires, and you can begin working in that direction with a new feeling of harmony with the whole of Ourself. Being aware of your deepest desires as Ourself will arouse a powerful confidence in your efforts to bring your most fundamental desires to life. As you proceed with manifesting your deepest desires, remember that you can always come back to this Reflection to re-prioritize where you want to be putting your time and energy. Going through this process will help lessen any doubts or insecurities you may have about what your most fundamental desires, or higher-desires, truly are.

If we take the time to thoroughly sort through our desires we will find that our deepest desires ultimately come from our primary identity, Ourself, and that they therefore have purpose and meaning beyond our individual selves; they connect us to and move the rest of Ourself in new ways. With this broader connection comes broader responsibility. Fulfilling your most fundamental desires will require you to really "be all that you can be." While at times this might seem overwhelmingly challenging, nothing will ever be as enduringly satisfying as developing the abilities of your essential nature as a unique aspect of Ourself. It becomes particularly exciting when you begin to see your efforts having a positive impact on the lives of others—either directly (as a helper, teacher, or performer) or indirectly through the improvements the process is having on your own emotional and cognitive well-being.

The word "guidance" has the implication of something separate from ourselves leading us, but what it really refers to is the process of sincerely acknowledging the wealth of feelings or impressions which continuously emerge from within Ourself to help us sort through our deepest desires. So rather than being led by something outside of ourselves, guidance is the experience of seeing through the façade of "me, myself, and I" clearly enough to recognize and feel the deeper insight and movement of Ourself. Finding ourselves in Ourself involves learning to recognize this inner guidance on a regular basis.

There is no way to successfully pretend your way through life. It hurts to live when you are disconnected psychically from Ourself, missing out on the guidance and opportunities that Ourself is so full of. Your life flies by day after day, and yet you don't feel like you have really been living. Carrying out the basic survival motions of daily life without also living out our higher-desires is like operating a conveyor belt with nothing on it—you're using energy to keep the belt moving, but to what end? It's what you put on the conveyor belt that makes it meaningful.

When we feel genuine excitement about an activity we need to have patience and perseverance as we begin to try our hand at it. Many people upon failing to do an activity well on their first try decide that they just aren't good at it, and therefore they are unwilling to try a second, third, fourth, and fifth time because they are too embarrassed to look awkward. The fear of failure is for humans perhaps the most powerful deterrent from fulfilling our true pursuits. We can't expect to be great at things the first few times we try. Any activity takes practice to develop.

Rather than focusing on whether or not you excel at something from the start, tune into how you feel when you do the activity. Does it just feel right? Are you naturally inspired to work hard developing at the activity? Do you enjoy practicing the activity even alone, blissfully losing track of time? These are the important criteria; it is a tragedy if we let our fears of failure stop us from pursuing an activity that could be a source of profound meaning and joy in our lives, and the lives of those around us.

If we can begin to realize that there really is no "me" to fail as we are all merely Ourself, then we can be more open and willing to try the activities that we are really interested in. Our mental concept of "me" is like a bulletin board to which we tack all of our memories of things we feel guilty, ashamed, or embarrassed about having done or not done, and a thousand excuses as to why we should not, or can not, do any given activity.

However, when your perception is opened by the recognition that you are only Ourself, the wind of Ourself will come blasting through you like a hurricane, and will begin to rip all of this mental paperwork off of the heavy bulletin board of the self. Finally we are free to participate in life without this wardrobe of negative and paralyzing mind junk. Ourself's energy, which has been so tied up, can begin to spin like the Tasmanian Devil; forever releasing the inner mashed potatoes which have been slowing us down for so long.

When we realize that everything everywhere is Ourself, we

find that attitudes and feelings which have formerly been limiting to us begin to appear both obvious and impotent. We will gradually notice that our hesitations, fears, and self-criticisms begin to seem flat or deflated. They may not disappear altogether, but as we recognize the smile of Ourself looking through our limiting emotions and thoughts they begin to lose their power over us, and start to resemble television advertisements—mere nuisances to be ignored.

While we practice and develop at the activities we are most passionate about we will notice that this process becomes like a screen through which we can more clearly experience the absurdity of our thinking, and through which Ourself can begin to communicate new feelings, understanding, and guidance to us. Sometimes these insights will be about the activity itself, sometimes about broader themes and patterns of Ourself that the activity serves as a metaphor for, and sometimes about unrelated questions that we have been mentally chewing on or obsessing over. When our conscious mind becomes fully engaged in an activity, it creates an opening in our psyche for the wide wisdom of Ourself to blow in through.

Through practicing any activity with open-minded integrity we are inevitably confronted by reality in challenging ways that stimulate and brighten the light of Ourself in our lives. This is why developing the meaningful activities of our lives as Ourself is one of the most effective way to break free from the strangling mental and emotional weeds that grow out of and around the busy monologue of "me, myself, and I." We must seize these opportunities life gifts us with to discover and outgrow limiting attitudes and emotional situations.

Unfortunately it can be hard to make it far enough along in the process of finding ourselves in Ourself to discover specifically which activities we are inspired to pursue and develop in our lives. It takes a great deal of willingness and action to explore the wide world of human activity, and to find what truly inspires or revives us. For many people, the mixed up notion that there must be one ultimate activity they are here to do blinds them to the varied responsibilities they have in this world.

Most of us have a range of activities we are here to develop, learn from, and share with others—from the simplest activities, such as brushing our teeth, to the more complex activities of work, service, artistic or personal expression, and various forms of recreation. It seems that a combination of laziness and fear inhibits many people from developing the wide array of possible interests which they could realistically pursue. As a result we have a very fragmented world where people narrowly identify themselves with one kind of hobby or profession, and we make a big fuss about people who are broader than that while labelling them a "renaissance" woman or man.

The truth of the matter is that having more than one passionate pursuit helps us to notice the connections between different activities. There is a web of interconnected phenomena within Ourself which we can only come to recognize and know firsthand through journeying down the road of real learning. These parallel patterns of Ourself become increasingly clear through practicing and developing at seemingly different activities because the deeper commonalities begin to reveal themselves. As these deeper commonalities become clearer and clearer we eventually become intimately familiar with the common thread in all activity—the primordial pattern of Ourself. This is perhaps the ultimate meaning of all human activity—to serve as a lens through which we can develop our awareness and understanding of the essential design of Ourself.

Some of the activities we love or are talented at might be income producing while others may have nothing to do with making money. Many of the activities we perform express essential parts of ourselves which if not expressed can cause our enthusiasm for life to whither away. As we face the many practical demands of our lives we also must exercise the parts of

53

ourselves which don't serve practical ends if we are to avoid becoming weighed down by depression. We have to keep ourselves thriving holistically as Ourself if we are to really thrive at all. We all need to maintain joy evoking, or "re-*creation*-al" activities in our lives to keep our sails full, and to help us through difficult or stressful times. Finding ourselves in Ourself requires us to look beyond practical considerations, and to trust that if we courageously and sincerely try to bring forth what Ourself has manifested us to do in this world, then Ourself will show us how to handle any necessary practical considerations along the way. We need to engage in an ongoing investigation into who we are, and what kinds of activities we need to be doing for the well-being of both our practical and impractical parts.

As we get to know what kinds of activities make Ourself purr within us we will find that there are certain unique qualities to the way we approach these activities which stand out from the way in which other people do them. This is like discovering your style as an artist, or your voice as a musician. As you discover the patterns which are unique to yourself you are discovering who you really are as Ourself. We each occupy an area within the whole of Ourself which has unique and recognizable patterns. This is how signatures work—everyone's signature has unique patterning which an expert can identify and recognize.

In fact, your signature is a good place to start searching for and uncovering the unique patterns of Ourself that you represent. Do you see elements of other people's signatures in your own? In other words, can you recognize certain qualities about your own signature which at some point in your life you remember imitating or incorporating into your own because you saw and liked these qualities in other people's signatures?

As you investigate your signature and all of your other traits with the clarity of Ourself, recognizing the layers of characteristics which have been adopted from the patterns of others, you will naturally begin to shed these inauthentic layers. This is not to say that you will no longer learn from or be influenced by others, but by being conscious of your influences as Ourself you will establish your own authentic ways of being and doing rather than unconsciously clinging to the safety of imitation.

As you become aware of yourself as Ourself you will also begin to notice elements of the way you walk that you incorporated or forged from other people. Try taking a long walk alone, and allow yourself to be completely aware of yourself as Ourself walking. Do you recognize other people's styles of walking in your own? Just allow yourself to be aware of it. The more you recognize all that is second-hand within yourself, the more you will find an authentic way of doing beginning to naturally emerge in your life. Artificial qualities will fall away like water droplets fall from a duck's oily feathers, thereby clarifying the many genuine ways in which you fit into the oeuvre of Ourself.

Though we will continue finding ourselves in Ourself throughout our lives as we grow and change, there is no reason to delay in taking steps towards manifesting Ourself *right now*. The fact that we can not immediately know all that we are here to do, or know everything that we might eventually want to develop in our lives, shouldn't distract us from the tasks at hand. We may not get to those other dimensions of our lives if we don't first develop the things we know to be important in our lives today.

If you have even one small dream or goal, then start working towards that and it will lead you into a broader pursuit than you realized. Everything in Ourself is interconnected, so if you can find even one authentic part of yourself, you can at least begin developing that, and it will inevitably bring you towards your larger purposes in this world; just as all little rivers eventually flow into bigger ones.

By discounting the validity of our interests and pursuits we eventually become depressed and hopeless. The birth of hope is the immediate consequence of action. As soon as we begin to act out our roles within Ourself—no matter how insignificant they might initially seem—we break the inertia of inactivity, and a positive sense of hope begins to grow in us which if nurtured and maintained will sustain us through the challenges we must face as we develop our lives. If we keep moving, making the effort to develop, and seeing through our fears and doubts with the one-thing-vision of Ourself, life is bound to continue to reveal to us the activities that will be most inspiring to ourselves as individuals, and to Ourself as a whole. This process of manifesting Ourself is the real carnival of life that is always ready and waiting for us to jump into!

Chapter 4

Manifesting Ourself

As we develop an ongoing awareness of what interests, abilities, or patterns are natural to us as parts of Ourself, an irresistible urge surfaces within us to begin manifesting all of this potential. When you give a seed the right environment and circumstances in which to sprout and grow, the previously dormant seed comes to life. It is the same with us—when we recognize the full spectrum of our aptitudes within the inspiring context of Ourself we begin to sprout and grow as we receive nourishment from the light, soil, and water of Ourself. Having explored our most fundamental desires and how they fit into the wider schema of Ourself, we are in a good place to begin taking steps towards fulfilling these higher-desires as Ourself.

In preparation, we may need to thoughtfully consider what steps will most efficiently move us towards our goals. This process of reflecting on specifically how our dreams will become realities is valuable in two ways. First of all it helps us to know where to begin putting our efforts in practical ways. Second, as we passionately visualize the manifestation of our higher-desires, we as parts of Ourself begin to pedal the wheels of Ourself which begin to influence circumstances to work in our favor as we proceed with action.

As we become more conscious of our true interests and talents we need to be willing to do the necessary work to develop these buds into blossoms. The process of developing your potentials into full blown abilities is one of the most important dimensions of manifesting Ourself. Manifesting Ourself requires us to develop fluency in the movements or language of the activities that we are passionate about. This fluency comes about through practice. For example, when you first try as a child to whistle or to snap your fingers it seems impossible. Yet you just keep trying, and after you've tried a hundred or two hundred times, you start to be able to do it.

Repetition is essential for learning because it is only through repetition that we can thoroughly familiarize ourselves with what works and what doesn't work. Repetition also allows us to encounter and experience the many subtle aspects of our minds and bodies which are involved in the particular action we are practicing. We have to remain open and flexible in this process because the experiential learning of Ourself rarely follows a straight line, but instead winds like a river. The wonderfully rich and endless learning process involved in developing any activity becomes a window to some of the most meaningful insights into Ourself we can experience. Learning is about much more than mental memorization of information; it is a multidimensional process which has no end, and is therefore an eternally reliable source of deep satisfaction and meaning.

However, the demands of such work frequently draw out our laziest aspects which can be paralyzing if we are unable to recognize that laziness is usually a mask worn by our fears and emotional resistances. While eating well and getting enough sleep can help us to generally be more energetic, freeing ourselves from limiting fears and draining emotional problems may be the *most* important step towards overcoming our own inertia.

Thus manifesting Ourself requires a lot of courage because we have to work through many different fragile and resistant parts of ourselves. This courage is to be found within the true perception of ourselves as Ourself. When we really see that everything within us, and beyond us, is all Ourself, we become aware that we are not only embraced by Ourself's infinite and implicit love, but we are also composed of this love. The more conscious we become of this, the more secure and courageous we become in facing the pains and supposed failures of our pasts, and similarly the more secure and courageous we become in taking risks in the present and future as we manifest Ourself.

In addition to realizing our desires, and initiating activities that match who we really are, manifesting Ourself also includes making changes in our personal lives which have a lightening and freeing effect on our lives. As you begin to encounter more genuine aspects of yourself through Ourself, you will feel the need to update the parts of your life that seem obsolete. Little by little you will be moved to work through, or revise, every aspect of your life, allowing it to be transformed by the developments coming through you from deep within Ourself.

A safe way to begin this process is to begin with small steps or small changes. As we begin taking meaningful little steps towards bringing our lives into tune with our true identity as Ourself, we will very quickly begin to see the profound influence small changes or steps can have. Big changes come about through little changes that we *follow through* with. All of Ourself grows and evolves through constant small changes and efforts which form a progression or story. As we recognize this happening in our lives we become aware of ourselves as Ourself *manifesting* Ourself. As this process develops momentum, our eagerness to discover the changes that each day will bring continually intensifies, just like the mounting anticipation one feels about reading each subsequent chapter of a novel one is enthralled with.

Reflection 4

Sit comfortably, breath naturally, and relax completely. Think of one of the higher-desires you came up with in the last Reflection—a desire which you can clearly see would really be beneficial to yourself, without harming others. Slowly embark on a visual journey of all the steps and stages involved in bringing this desire to life. Confidently visualize each step as though it has already happened, like a memory, engaging your feelings in the visualization process. Let your visualization be as detailed and thorough as you can make it, trying to achieve a very realistic sense of what is involved in manifesting your higher-desire.

When you get to steps which you have doubts about, or which seem impossible to you, orient yourself especially strongly to the sense that you are remembering things that have already transpired, so that the seemingly insurmountable challenges will appear to have been already resolved through Ourself's invisible hand which has the capacity to work all kinds of surprising graces.

In literary terms this is referred to as, "willing suspension of disbelief," and in this case it is an important practice as it allows you to keep up your momentum rather than letting your fears slow you down. Keeping up your momentum and optimism in turn helps Ourself to keep moving in your favor. Much like a placebo effect, if you believe challenges will be overcome, it helps Ourself to actually overcome potential challenges.

As your desire becomes fully realized, really explore the feelings which accompany this. In addition to feeling your own joy and satisfaction, feel the joy your realized desire brings to others. This might be because your desire has a direct benefit to others, or it might simply be that in your becoming more whole and complete as Ourself, the good vibrations you emit as a result inspire, or help light the way for others to do the same. The more tangibly you feel all of this, the more deeply integrated with Ourself your desire will become.

The more you experience your desire as Ourself's desire, the more powerful the motivation will be to continue taking steps towards realizing your desire, and similarly, the more Ourself will move in a way that helps circumstances to work with you instead of against you. Though there will likely be challenges *along the way, you have both the motivation to do what must be done, and the confidence and support of Ourself to help you along the way. Revisit this Reflection regularly as you begin to make changes in your life; especially as you encounter obstacles. By regularly visualizing everything working out, and simultaneously taking any practical or obvious steps that you need to take towards manifesting your desire, you will guide the inevitable change of Ourself in the direction of your desire.*

What if things don't seem to be going the way we want them to? What if the fruit of our labor turns out to be apples when we thought we were growing pears? Because you are engaging with our primordial identity, Ourself, you are sure to encounter mysteries and truths that are difficult to understand with the mind. Sometimes we have to follow in hot pursuit of one desire so that a different manifestation of Ourself can come into being. Sometimes we may not foresee the situations or circumstances which we are creating as we take steps towards manifesting a desire. We might not notice until later that as a result things have worked out in beneficial ways beyond what we could have foreseen or imagined possible.

Ultimately we can do nothing but trust Ourself as we work our way towards what we can see of our higher-desires. If you have ever climbed a mountain, then you know the comparable experience of continuously thinking you see the top of the mountain just ahead, only to realize when you get to that point that you can now see new higher ground ahead. Yet you trust that eventually you *really will* reach the top, and of course you eventually do!

In some cases there may be problems with what we desire that we are unable to anticipate, which reality can only reveal to us gradually as we make efforts towards our goal. As we are confronted by such discrepancies between reality and our expectations we have to learn to view these in a positive light so that if things do not seem to be working the way we want them to we don't get paralyzed by a sense of failure. Meaningful journeys are willy-nilly, and full of wonder and surprises—some to our liking, and some not, but all of which stretch and expand our narrowness, and deepen our awareness of Ourself. Not every endeavor will go the way we planned, but if our intentions are in harmony with Ourself all along the way, then we will find our way to a satisfying ending—even if it is not the ending we originally envisioned.

So far we have been discussing manifesting Ourself as realizing our deepest desires, or getting from point A to point B. However, there is another, equally important dimension to manifesting Ourself which is not about results, but is instead about process. Process is the total experience of doing; which becomes infinitely richer when we are aware of ourselves and everything else as Ourself. Our awareness of the total process of Ourself "doing" everything all at once exposes us to the real meaning of life.

This deep experience of the eternal action of the whole of Ourself has a distinct quality best described as constant *creative development*.

In an attempt to better capture this "real meaning of life," I'd like to relay a quasi-creation myth of sorts. This is the story of Onechild constantly improving its situation. Onechild is synonymous with Ourself, and it is descriptive of the fact that as an absolute and singular whole Ourself is like a lonely child who in the beginning... began to play—and of course never stopped! Onechild is all that has ever been, and all that will ever be. In Onechild's solitude, Onechild has inevitably been moved to create games to play by itself as a child will do if left alone in a sandbox, or in a room full of toys. Since Onechild had no toys, Onechild began to feel itself into the infinite variety of forms that exist within reality—including all of us individuals, all that we know in the world, and everything else that happens to be real anywhere and everywhere.

The games Onechild creates within itself involve all kinds of drama, action, suffering, ugliness, beauty, and humor. As a result we might not like all that we find ourselves going through as aspects of Onechild. We are bound to encounter Onechild's loneliness and Onechild's pain in our lives, as well as Onechild's joy. At times the tragic injustices we all must witness or personally face can be incredibly difficult to bear, but clearly there is no way to completely avoid such challenges. The infinite and eternal playground of Onechild that we all exist within is the gateway to understanding the total gamut of our own feelings and experiences because we *are all actually* Onechild, and therefore the spectrum of our feelings and experiences is a reflection of the spectrum of Onechild's feelings and experiences. This is the meaning of the statement, "God created man in his own image." It's true that the essential patterns and qualities of the creator are to be found throughout this creation that we are all part of.

We have to keep this in mind as we make our way through life's ups and downs because it helps us to see that we are not Onechild's victims—we are Onechild itself! When we feel overcome with loneliness we need to let go of the sense that it is exclusively *our* loneliness. What we are really feeling is the eternal loneliness of Onechild which we are part of, and have been manifested from. If we can let go of our sense of isolation from everything else, and begin to experience both the pain and joy of our lives as expressions of our own true nature as Onechild, we will begin to experience our lives as notes within the whole of Onechild's diverse symphony.

The reason it is so important to really "get" the basic message of this admittedly oversimplified story of Onechild is so that we won't spend our entire lives stuck in the victim mentality that is so prevalent; and in a way inevitable from the fragmented perpsective of "me, myself, and I." Our pain is Ourself's pain, so there is no sense in feeling like a victim—the raw deals we get handed in life are reflections of the raw deal that Ourself has always been faced with that is simply the nature of reality itself. We can't escape it because we are all Ourself, and this pain is a natural dimension of Ourself that we have to know if we are to really know Ourself. The expression, "If you can't get out of it, then get into it," comes to mind; what else can we really do? What else can Ourself do?

Ourself does get into it; it creates and it develops. Onechild's basic eternal process of creative development, or constantly improving its situation, *is* the meaning of life. Creative development was and continues to be Onechild's proactive response to its seemingly bleak situation, and we were all familiar with this process at some point in our lives. From the moment we were born we engaged in this practice: learning to move, pick things up, crawl, and communicate. Every stage of our lives involves new stages of such creative development. This is the fundamental action of intelligence. It is the fundamental action of all of Onechild entertaining and nurturing itself.

As we return to engaging in this process as Ourself—whether in the form of cooking, brushing our teeth, or learning to hit a golf ball—we are allowed the incredible opportunity to taste this eternal pastime of Onechild. As we expand the activities of our lives through the rich mix of repetition and innovation that is at the heart of creative development, we develop an intimacy and familiarity with this primordial action of Onechild that some have referred to as "God the verb." As we develop competence in the subtle nuances of whatever activities we are working on, we discover the incredible patterns, inner structures, and archetypal truths that exist within the creations of Onechild.

Deepening our familiarity with the personality and feeling of our common original nature, Onechild, through engaging in the process of creative development is the ultimate value and blessing of manifesting Ourself. We most deeply access intimacy with ourselves as Ourself through action. In silence and stillness we can be soothed and healed by Ourself, but it is in the constant discovery of creative development that we experience the full power and intelligence of Ourself. Through experiencing the joys and benefits of engaging with Ourself in action, we develop a zest for life that can lead to real success in our lives—success not based solely on wealth or the opinions of others, but based on the absolute richness of our own experience.

Through practice and consistent small efforts we make our way through higher, broader, and more ecstatic dimensions of Ourself. As we engage in this work we encounter parts of ourselves which are resistant to both the changes that we find necessary, and the enormous dedication and effort required to learn how to fully manifest our patterns. We need a great deal of willingness and integrity to move through the many emotional and psychological blocks which disrupt the learning process, and hold us back from successfully manifesting Ourself. In the process, we grow and evolve inwardly as we develop our lives outwardly. This work is never really done—there is no end to the process of refining your unique patterns, growing through resistances, and manifesting the multiple aspects of Ourself that you are. As we become accustomed to the eternal process of manifesting Ourself we begin to witness our lives as aspects of Onechild's all-encompassing, ongoing work of art.

Manifesting Ourself is comparable to adjusting the antennae and dial on a radio in an effort to improve the reception. As you become aware of ways of doing, and ways of being that aren't efficient, productive, or authentic you spontaneously adjust, and the reception of the eternal song of Ourself becomes clearer and clearer in your life. Whether the radio's static has been the result of your strategy of attempting to accomplish a goal, the result of poor form in your way of executing an activity, or the result of something about your persona that doesn't really fit—such as a hairstyle that just isn't you—the static can be cleared up through Ourself's process of creative development. This process is the spontaneous response of recognizing the source of the static. When you really see what's not working in your approach to doing or being the cure emerges naturally from within Ourself.

It's like calling someone who has their back turned towards you—when they hear their name called they automatically turn to face you. When we identify a problem our natural intelligence as Ourself calls forth solutions which we can recognize if we are open minded, and listening for the guidance of Ourself. This process of discovery is very exciting—there is nothing quite so satisfying as recognizing a problem, and then understanding or seeing the solution spontaneously from within. You encounter a new kind of confidence when you become a first-hand kind of person by recognizing and resolving the many sources of static in your life through your own insight and resourcefulness as part of Ourself.

Hence, one key to manifesting Ourself is developing a productively critical eye for which aspects of our persona, and which ways of approaching a goal or doing an activity are not serving us very well. By clearly and honestly noticing the static in our reception and what lies behind it, the doors of insight open to us, unveiling obvious alternatives. Then we just need to be willing to follow through with the changes that we recognize as solutions. If we are truly willing to follow through, we can start to powerfully manifest Ourself in our lives through very simple actions; constantly improving our situation as part of Onechild's eternal pastime.

For example, if the static in your reception is the result of a job you're unhappy doing, then you begin taking obvious steps—such as keeping your eyes open for other jobs, updating your resume, and reflecting on what kind of work, people, and environment you would like a new job to include. If you recognize that you are lacking certain skills you would need for such a job, then you naturally begin looking into how you can acquire these skills. Ourself's process of creative development is the means by which you can work gradually towards realizing your most vital hopes. Of course there are no guarantees that our future life will fit an exact mold of what we think we want it to be like, but what is certain is that if we engage with our life fully as Ourself— courageously, patiently, and diligently taking the necessary small steps—then our lives will move and evolve in the right direction for our overall well-being.

If the static in our reception is the result of poor form in an activity we are practicing, say for example in learning the piano you are not using the right fingering to move from the bridge of a song back into the verse resulting in a rough sounding transition, then you have to slow way down, and really critically observe how you are executing the fingering. When you recognize what is awkward about the fingering you're using, you will concurrently understand a more fluid alternative. Then, to follow through, you might have to slowly practice the new and improved fingering over and over until you have really outgrown the awkward fingering. Manifesting Ourself always involves this sequence of productive critical insight, recognition of problems, understanding of solutions, and finally slow, diligent practice.

As you begin to develop each of the activities that make up your life, you will find that the qualities required to do one activity well, relate to the other activities also. For example, qualities such as concentration, patience, attention to detail, and endurance are important in every kind of activity that humans perform. So when you are practicing and developing one activity, you are simultaneously improving at all the other activities in your life by deepening your understanding of and relationship to "doing" in general.

Lastly, if the static in your reception of Ourself is the result of some aspect of your persona—say for example you have never liked your name because you don't feel like it actually fits who you are—then again, to clear up the static you must fully recognize the problem, be open to perceiving the alternative, and then be willing to follow through with the changes that begin to come about through your insight. Making changes of this nature—changes in your outer persona which begin to create greater harmony with your growing awareness of who you really are—can have a profoundly freeing affect on your life. This is analogous to the cinematic cliché where the studious female's glasses are removed, her hair is let down from a tight bun, and she is unveiled as the woman of elegantly beautiful splendor she really is.

As we have moved through our lives in this world, which is full of so many pressures, most of us have adopted or had put upon us patterns which either do not suit who we really are, or do not allow us to thrive. Whether these patterns concern our career choices, our ways of doing an activity, or our persona we can begin to recognize them as we find out who we really are through our deepening awareness of ourselves as Ourself. As we become aware of these distortions to our authenticity we find that we really can not evade making changes—the recognition itself is transformative and catalytic. If we are really going to move forward in our lives we must have confidence in our insight into the causes of static in our lives, profoundly acknowledge to ourselves as Ourself that these are no longer viable options, and discern that the changes we need to make are unavoidable.

Every little pattern which doesn't match the patterns that are truly natural to you, and has been allowed to cover up your real patterns, is like a ball and chain to manifesting Ourself. If you let enough incompatible patterns remain part of your life, then you eventually find yourself inwardly paralyzed. In contrast, every change that you recognize as having the potential to decrease the static in your life, which you then follow through with changing, enriches and enlivens your life and deepens your sense of harmony with your true identity as Ourself.

Really manifesting Ourself requires us to have the courage to leave behind all the aspects of ourselves that we recognize as incompatible with who we have found ourselves to be in Ourself. Of course, we can't do this all at once. We have to develop and maintain a healthy rhythm for ourselves to dance to. We have to make changes at a pace that doesn't disrupt the productive or positive flow of our lives and relationships. The "one day at a time" approach is helpful in this process—actually "one moment at a time" is more like it. Similar to a short order cook, we can only take the orders as they come; if we worry about how we are going to do later orders, we will mess up the ones we are working on in the present. However, part of the complexity of manifesting Ourself is that we don't get to respond to orders that come in a clear chronological progression—it is up to us to do the prioritizing. If we become overwhelmed by the myriad steps we are aware we need to take to manifest Ourself, then we can get stuck and become unproductive.

In Reflection number 3 we explored what our top three desires were; we can revisit that Reflection process often to help us to prioritize our higher-desires. The main thing however, is to just keep moving while trusting Ourself to do the real organizing and planning, rather than getting stuck in obsessing over exactly what you are doing, and why. The supposed importance of "time management" really boils down to this: stay in touch with Ourself as you walk forward, and learn to depend on your intuitive measure of quality to determine what is a waste of time versus what is an important step forward, or an important diversion or resting point. We can start by taking small steps forward towards our higher-desires, or by making little changes in our lives that seem to come naturally, and as our experience of manifesting Ourself further broadens and deepens we will rapidly find our way to bigger changes and developments.

A good place to initiate change in a way that is hopefully nonthreatening to yourself, or to the people you are close to, is to simply start a new recreational or artistic activity. Start playing a sport you've always wanted to play, learning to cook a kind of food you've always wanted to know how to cook, or start playing an instrument you've always wanted to know how to play.

Throw out *all* ideas about why you "just can't" do a particular activity—if you need to, make a list of these reasons, and then begin problem solving how to overcome each of them. If some of these obstacles seem insurmountable, then try to accept that sometimes we have to just have a little faith. We can not always have the luxury of security as we manifest Ourself. We sometimes have to just go for it. If we take the first step towards doing an activity that we really care about, then circumstances are sure to begin to budge a little in our favor; and then a little more with each subsequent step we take as Ourself.

However, be careful not to deceive yourself that you are taking steps by simply spending money on new equipment or "how to" books. Instead find the quickest way to actually begin the "doing" of the activity itself. You might find that if you start with the "doing," the necessary equipment or instruction will find its way to you as you go, without having to spend lots of money. When you are sincerely trying to manifest your true patterns as Ourself, help will come in all sorts of surprising ways. This is the way of Ourself; again reminiscent of the saying "God helps those who help themselves." Don't measure change in your life by what you have bought, but instead by what you *actually do* each day as Ourself. Similarly, value the aid you get from people and circumstances along the way as affirmations that what you are working on is really in harmony with Ourself.

By the time you have really initiated a new activity, or have started working through the aspects of your personal life you desire change in, you will begin to notice a growing enthusiasm and trust in Ourself's process of creative development. This is Ourself's healthy addiction—Onechild's original addiction to constantly improving its situation, which continues to be the underlying rhyme and reason to all that is beautiful and authentic in the world.

While moving beyond contemplation and into action is the main thrust of manifesting Ourself, it is important to note that sometimes improving your situation will mean taking a break, taking a nap, or goofing off. We need to take care of *all* of our parts if we are to truly thrive; this includes honoring our need for rest, introspection, pleasure, love, and "re-creation." We need to make sure that we don't devalue the parts of us that are not about outer achievement or making money.

For example, we might need to hit a tennis ball against a backboard for an hour a day; not because we are training to play competitively, but because during that hour we work through difficult or aggressive emotions we are experiencing—what a friend of mine called "emotional tooth-brushing." Activities like this—other examples are learning to read music, drawing from life, cooking, or learning to throw pottery on a wheel—that involve interacting with reality in a direct and unforgiving way provide us with a sort of consciousness massage which puts us on the same wavelength as reality; thereby making it easier to recognize the beauty of Ourself that we are all part of, and giving us a needed break from the various obsessions of our overbearing minds.

As we make significant changes in *what* we choose to spend our time doing, and in *how we go about* doing things, a great deal of friction can be generated both within ourselves between the old and the new, and between ourselves and other people that we are close to who may not be as happy about the changes in our lives as we are. The important thing is that we be aware of ourselves as Ourself, and that we be very clear about the fact that the changes we are making are coming from a pure place.

In making changes towards really being Ourself we aren't trying to be radical, we are just trying to be true to who and what we really are. So don't let people bully you around by acting like you're just causing trouble as you begin to change yourself, and the world around you. The people who are causing trouble are the people who are *resisting* all the positive changes we can each make in ourselves and the world! Manifesting Ourself is the true work and responsibility of *all* human beings. It includes every kind of human activity, and every dimension of our lives. We each have to be open to whatever roles Ourself has for us—or *has us for*. It's like when you audition for a play; you don't know what role you might be cast for. You just have to accept whatever role you get, and make the most of it by giving it your best effort.

Many of the duties we find ourselves having in this life are not pleasant. We need to be careful that we don't delude ourselves into thinking we are "getting a life" by eliminating everything unpleasant or difficult from our lives. Manifesting Ourself almost always involves difficult and challenging work and situations. You will receive guidance and help along the way, but this doesn't mean it will be easy or enjoyable all the time.

We are also sure to encounter much ambiguity and uncertainty on this journey; we can't always pre-discern the ways in which we must grow and be stretched in order to manifest our uniquely authentic patterns as Ourself. Life will always remain mysterious to human beings because we can never see and know everything in the same way that Ourself as a whole is conscious of itself. However, we can be aware of ourselves and all that we encounter in our lives as Ourself, and this will help us to understand, on at least an as-needed basis, the meaning behind the various experiences we all must go through.

The words "just enough" capture this minimalist quality of the inner guidance and understanding we each must rely on to manifest Ourself; there is a natural back and forth interaction between understanding and action. If we lose the balance between them the focus of our work will stray. It's like when an artist is drawing an object: if they draw too much without glancing back up at the object, then they lose track of what it is they are really drawing, but if they spend too much time studying the object without making marks on the drawing, then they fail to manifest the visual information they are gathering into their drawing. As we come to trust this "just enough" guidance and understanding, and to consistently act on it, the changes we are making in our lives will eventually bring us to the miraculous state of being blissfully conscious that everything in our lives is happening as Ourself, with Ourself, and from Ourself.

If everybody in the world—or even half the people in the world—were to live in such a powerful and authentic way, the abundance of joy, intelligence, love and peace in this world would be so overflowing that we could surely solve the problems which we, the human family, are currently so overwhelmed with. This is the real world peace we are hopefully all working towards—a world where people are freely thriving as parts of one whole. To move the world in this direction, more of us need to start being Ourself, manifesting Ourself, and most importantly, exalting in Ourself.

Chapter 5

Exalting in Ourself

Our word "exalt" comes from the Latin word *exaltare* which means to raise or elevate. As we increasingly become exposed to the awesome scope and profound implications of Ourself, an upwardly spiraling pulse is awakened in us which seeks expression through movement and sound. Having recognized our true condition as parts of Ourself, we now begin to experience the marvel, cleansing, and bliss of *exalting* in Ourself. This ecstatic awakening to the elevating inner motion of Ourself leads us through every color of the feeling spectrum, from the most painful and heavy up through the most joyful and light.

The innately positive result of walking, crying, singing, dancing, and laughing our way up through this range of feeling is that the damp heaviness of our feelings begins to air out in the wind of Ourself, and as a result we start to genuinely lighten up. To "lighten up" is to be raised into the vast altitudes of Ourself where freedom is the only rule, and the answers to the gnawing questions of our soul are to be found far beyond our mind's capacity to "know."

As we exalt in Ourself every aspect of our heart, mind, body, and soul begins to break free from the frigid illusion of separateness, and is released by the warmth and vibrancy of Ourself into the natural and free movement of Ourself—like ice on a thawing river in the spring loudly breaking apart and flowing downstream. We need to welcome and take responsibility for the feelings that surface in this process. Like children, our feelings need to be heard and seen, and given a chance to express themselves. If given this space our feelings can come into full bloom; providing us with the ongoing opportunity to gain deeper insight into the real nature of our feelings. This is how we develop emotional and spiritual health in our lives.

Though everything *is* Ourself, everything *is not* homogeneous. Ourself is not the absence of distinct qualities; it is the elemental quality that all things share in common. The infinite forms of Ourself display a plethora of qualities—some finer and some coarser—and the same is true of our thoughts, feelings, and intentions. Developing our sensitivity to the different qualities of Ourself is critical for our well-being. Being sensitive to what is fine and what is coarse in ourselves allows us to distinguish between qualities worth cultivating, and qualities to be cautious of.

The unique combination of qualities each of us embodies we refer to as our "character." Character is not static or permanent, but rather is constantly in flux and vulnerable to change, either for better or for worse. If we are strongly committed to resisting the perpetual change of our individual character, then we create a dangerous state of soul constipation. While this stagnation might be helpful in our effort to convince ourselves and each other that we are separate and stable creatures, in the end it inevitably leads to sickness.

If, on the other hand, we are strongly committed to being conscious of the fluidity and impermanency of our character, and in being moved and uplifted through our consciousness of Ourself, then we can experience a life full of the inner riches of Ourself's finest qualities and blessings. We all have a choice—in our feelings we can remain in a coarse state of muddy inertia, or we can lighten up by allowing ourselves to be moved from within through our liberating awareness of Ourself.

This is why it is so critical that we manifest Ourself—it is through the creative development of our own interests and activities that we become intimately familiar with the different qualities of Ourself in action. We encounter finer dimensions of feeling as we lighten up in Ourself which enable us to flow with the "doing" of any activity like never before. Successfully manifesting Ourself ultimately relies on, and therefore develops, our fundamental capacity to exalt in Ourself.

In addition to exalting in Ourself as we manifest Ourself, we can also exalt in Ourself as an end in itself—as a process of worship or meditation. This helps the light of Ourself to radiate into every dark corner of our feelings, and the gust of Ourself to turn every part of ourselves like pinwheels. Over time this helps our character to develop in new and unexpected ways that eventually come to reflect Ourself's highest qualities. In essence this process of worship or meditation is a state of pure improvisation or spontaneity. Actors, dancers, artists, and musicians throughout time have practiced this improvisational approach to creating art which reflects the indefinable beauty of the unknown. When we lighten up and allow ourselves to be moved freely from within, we too experience the wisdom, culture, and cleansing of the ever-flowing, creative fountain of Ourself.

Have you ever jumped into a lake on a hot day, let out a holler of ecstasy, and just allowed yourself to move freely in the water? Somehow the weightless quality of floating in the water awakens in us an urge to move gracefully and spontaneously like soaring dancers twisting, stretching, and reaching our way through an endless, gravity-free sky.

Through the awareness that you truly are everything comes an unforeseeable release into an ocean of feeling where you can allow yourself to move and make sounds in a completely liberated way; letting go of socially acceptable facial and bodily composure, and allowing yourself to be moved by the naturally unfolding motion which is eternally emerging from the depths of Ourself. As you allow this unfolding motion to proceed through the totally free movement of your body and voice, you will experience the cathartic release of what may feel like lifetimes of tension, anxiety, and emotion. Through this catharsis a genuine sense of hope and wellness will begin to ripen in your feelings.

The recognition of your true identity, Ourself, is the portal through which you can be released from the rigidifying sense of responsibility and control which your mind usually exerts over your body. To be moved in this way from the waters of the infinite well of Ourself is the ultimate bliss and cleansing. The free movement of every aspect of your being as you lighten up in Ourself is the foundation of true inner and outer health.

Reflection 5

Find a quiet and private place where you feel totally safe to allow yourself to really be Ourself. Stand calmly, and let go of any tension in your body or feelings. Ignore your mind's incessant demands for your undivided attention, and be aware of your thoughts as reality simply thinking to itself. Freely sigh or moan as you exhale, and continue to relax your entire body allowing your eyes to close or open at any time. Openly and fully experience any feelings that well up in you as you let go—feelings which you may have been holding back because they are uncomfortable, or perhaps pleasant and familiar feelings of innocence forgotten in childhood. Allow yourself to express these feelings in any way you are compelled to, whether it involves moving, laughing, singing, shouting, crying, or venerating. Total freedom is the only rule here, and it is critical! Continue letting feelings and movement emerge from deep within your fundamental identity, Ourself. Continue to allow yourself to move and make sound in whatever ways you feel naturally impelled to. If you are not moved to express anything, then revel in the profound silence of Ourself, and just FEEL!

Be aware of the feelings not just in your heart or core, but throughout your body from your teeth through your head, down your back and out your arms, and down through your legs and into your toes. As you become conscious of tensions throughout your body, you might be overcome with the urge to start stretching, or swinging your arms, or even to start jumping, spinning, or bouncing. Don't resist—just move freely with any urge that arises from Ourself. When you engage in this spontaneous inner dance of Ourself you never know what you will encounter, but you can be sure that anything that comes out or through you in this relaxed state is something you ultimately need to feel or express. So enthusiastically follow your body's impulses without judging what you are doing.

The movement or sounds you are making might be gentle like a warm, fragrant spring breeze whispering through you, or they might more closely resemble a powerful waterfall crashing through you. Either way, you are experiencing the inner shower of Ourself— a spiritually and emotionally cleansing process of release and celebration. This is not a Reflection to just visit once or twice, this is the most thorough and important process of healing and rejuvenation we can engage in, and we should therefore lighten up as Ourself a little bit every day. It is an experience of absolute freedom from the burden of maintaining our mask of social composure, and instead allowing ourselves to bask and wriggle in our original nature as Ourself.

How did that feel? Refreshing? Enlivening? There is nothing more ecstatic than the true inner movement of Ourself washing through us. It sort of feels like we are a Push-Up popsicle with Ourself gently pushing up the contents of our inner congestion, and as we move these contents are both expressed and released through our movements. It is also like the glove analogy from Chapter 3—like the hand of Ourself reaches into us in a way we may not have felt since childhood, and begins to move us in ways that we may not understand the significance of with our minds, but which feel wonderful and healing to our soul.

If you didn't feel much this first time, then don't worry about it, but *do* keep practicing this inner release of freely lightening up in Ourself. As you continue to practice it, and accustom yourself to really letting go of your self-composure, fears, and hesitations, you will experience a deeper and deeper sense of release and exaltation. In the process you will come to recognize with increasing clarity all that is fine, and all that is coarse within you; enabling you to live your life from the higher atmosphere of Ourself.

It seems strange to me that we are not all accustomed to this process already. Why do many of us perceive such a natural process of inner restoration as being somehow esoteric or foreign? Is it because we are overly shy about our authentic feelings—having undoubtedly been shamed throughout our lives when we were really honest or open with others? Are we too embarrassed to enjoy moving and making sound freely because it lacks sophistication and glamour? Does it seem too infantile? Is it not intellectual enough? This is precisely the importance of exalting freely in Ourself—we all *do* have a non-intellectual (but richly intelligent) and infantile (but deeply complex), feeling core that needs to move and express itself in an unregulated way.

If we are embarrassed by this process, then we can keep it private, but we can't simply abandon our inner freedom because of the judgments of ourselves or others. If we all engaged in this kind of process more often—made it part of our daily routines like bathing or getting dressed—it would cease to feel so unusual. If we all regularly lightened up, and moved freely from within Ourself, wouldn't we be a much healthier and happier human race?

When we feel closed up inside and isolated from the rest of Ourself, it leads to a kind of inner paralysis, and the results are obviously very negative for our mental, physical, and spiritual well-being. In other words, when self-isolation overtakes our feelings, and the natural motion of Ourself within us is inhibited, we find that our feelings become heavier and heavier, and along with that heaviness comes malady of body, mind, and soul.

In contrast, when we freely exalt in Ourself all of our systems open up, start moving, and begin to be cleared out. For most of us, there are very few moments in the course of a day—or in the course of our whole lives for that matter—when we feel completely free in this way. Even when we *are not* in the presence of others, most of us feel compelled to maintain a socially acceptable poise which includes "appropriate" body postures, facial postures, and even psychological postures—all of which require a clenching down on our natural flow as parts of Ourself, with disastrous consequences for both our mental and physical health.

Though we are all vulnerable to health problems which are beyond our control, we can maximize our health potential by making a deep commitment within ourselves to lightening up and being profoundly free in Ourself. If we succumb to our fundamental lack of control with total willingness to be what we truly are as Ourself, and put forth intense effort in whatever ways we are guided to move, then we can experience a broad harmony with the whole of Ourself.

This is the only way to develop real inner calm. A sedentary or lazy life isn't a relaxing one. When we are sedentary or lazy, we become full of anxiety because something inside us knows we aren't living out the bountiful guidance of Ourself. It is through the movement of exalting in and manifesting Ourself that our anxious nerves are washed clean. Most of what ends up being meaningful in life does require intense effort and persistence to achieve. It is therefore critical to be able to stick to the tasks Ourself guides us into; even when we feel that we are at times being pushed beyond what we think we can handle. The more we accustom ourselves to following through with Ourself's guidance, the more we come to trust in our capacity to make it through those challenging moments that we are all inevitably confronted by where we just feel like quitting.

This is not to say that we don't also need stillness or rest in our lives. Rest is necessary because certain kinds of healing motion are very fine and subtle, and require stillness to occur. Obviously staying healthy does require a *balance* of action and healing rest; we just need to sincerely listen to our guidance about when to act and when to rest, and resist the temptation to merely give up whenever the going gets tough. On the other hand, some of us become so accustomed to pushing ourselves forward all the time that we forget to listen to Ourself's guidance to take a break or play a little. We are each the expert on our own selves, and if we are honest with ourselves we will find the guidance within Ourself concerning when to work, rest, and play so that we can keep our lives balanced and flowing as Ourself.

To really be healthy we must allow Ourself's guidance to freely move every aspect of our being, like the inner gears and components of a clock. This involves regularly exalting in Ourself in the way we practiced in this chapter's Reflection, and also keeping alive the many recreational activities of our lives which may not be productive towards any material end, but are certainly productive in the sense that they are restorative to our well-being as they each exercise different parts of ourselves that atrophy if not given the opportunity to move. We all have day to day lives we have to struggle to keep up with, but with a little creativity we can find ways within the busy frameworks of our lives to allow for the healing and revitalizing movement of our many parts. Exalting in Ourself fills us with the steam to keep our engines whistling so that we can maintain the motivation and courage we need to keep the different parts of ourselves being moved and developed in accordance with the guidance of Ourself—often in ways beyond our mind's comprehension.

The highest dimensions of Ourself are beyond our ability to conceive of. Human portrayals of the heavens, such as Renaissance paintings of winged angels and pink clouds, are attempts to poetically suggest to the imagination the nature of the beauty and divinity which exist within Ourself. Similarly, scenes in such paintings of prophets with hands lifted to the sky and open mouths emitting sacred utterances are attempts to depict people lightening up and exalting in the all inclusive creation of Ourself. We should always be open in our feelings to these higher or finer dimensions of Ourself, and the rapture that comes so naturally when we relax into the sacred wholeness of reality.

It is likely that most of Ourself will remain an immense mystery to our thinking minds, and therefore if we do not want to get stuck in our lives, then we ought not get too hung up on "knowing." Real understanding comes about through movement, whether it is the movement of conversation, exercise, writing, or freely exalting in Ourself.

Without opening ourselves up to the free movement and feelings that come through exalting in Ourself, we can never really "get a life." Getting a life is a spontaneous process that we have to make space for by seeing through the illusory monologue of "me, myself, and I," which is a heavy psychological composite of all our problems, fears, and doubts. When we let go of this by recognizing the face of Ourself dwelling within it all, then we begin to receive a deeper and clearer awareness of who we truly are as unique aspects of the whole, and to be moved from within in accordance with our uniqueness.

The point is to get unstuck, and to stay unstuck. It takes profound dedication not to fall into the inertia of those around you, or of your own comfort zone of separate identity. This is the eternal work of the spiritual life—recognizing that you *are* the whole, and in that recognition being exposed to and moved by the vibrant inner waves of Ourself. Just like a ball of clay that must first be wedged or kneaded to become workable and ready to create with, our consciousness needs to be regularly kneaded by Ourself if we are to remain supple and able to flow in harmony with the rest of Ourself. Exalting in Ourself is giving Ourself this opportunity to knead us from the inside out.

All we have to do is give this process the necessary time and space. It is helpful to have a somewhat private atmosphere where we won't be interrupted for anywhere from a few minutes to an hour. The rest happens by itself as we recognize that we are Ourself, and we allow ourselves to lighten up and exalt. As we become accustomed to being moved so freely from within, we eventually become comfortable feeling this inner movement of Ourself wherever we are.

Though it is cleansing and renewing to allow the process to move us at full tilt, it can also be extremely soothing and grounding to feel the subtle dance of Ourself quietly moving within us in the wide variety of settings we each must move through every day. Feeling this thread of life that moves through us as parts of Ourself is the survival tool we all need in order to face life's challenges, so the more comfortable we become with the sensation of Ourself pulsing within us the better.

It's okay to be dependent on Ourself. This is the healthy dependency we all share in common; it is really Ourself's dependency on itself—a sort of holistic "self-reliance." If we ignore this fundamental need to remember our primordial origin and fundamental identity, Ourself, and to allow ourselves to be lifted, cleansed, and healed by its motion, then we find ourselves constantly grasping at pieces rather than the whole. This constant grasping leads to a variety of dependencies that in the end tend to be very destructive to both our own life, and the lives of the people who love and care about us. The exit from this destructive isolation lies in allowing ourselves *to really be reality* in 3-D, exalting in the fathomless depths and heights of Ourself.

Chapter 6

Ourself in Relationship with Ourself

The fundamental premise or assumption we unconsciously cling to as we interact with other people is that we are each innately separate beings. If we were to discard this assumption, and enter into every social encounter with the awareness that we are actually all aspects of one whole interacting with Ourself, then we would enter into a totally different kind of relationship with one another. In realizing that "others" *actually are* Ourself we make real for the first time in our lives the notion, "Love thy neighbor as thyself," and thereby enter into the dawn of world peace.

When humanity begins to function as one harmonious whole through its recognition that we are all one thing, then the flower of peace will finally be allowed to blossom throughout this world. Of course that idealized moment will only come about through each one of us looking deeply and critically at what we are as individuals (aspects of Ourself), and who we are in our relationships with others (aspects of Ourself interacting with other aspects of Ourself). While we might like to think that simply becoming aware that we are all Ourself will instantaneously make our relationships easy or "perfect," this will likely not be the case.

However, as our one-thing-vision expands and deepens, our relationships become richly padded with the shock absorption of Ourself. The healing and calming nature of Ourself is the tool we need to begin working through the complex layers of racism, sexism, nationalism, ageism, classism and bariatricism (my word for oppressive prejudice towards overweight individuals) that keep our world so profoundly full of injustice and conflict. While awareness of our common nature and source, Ourself, provides us with the means to approach these difficult issues it will not spontaneously resolve these issues if we do not engage one another in this international healing work.

In almost every relationship there will be times when our awareness of Ourself will be pushed around and stretched by complexity, struggle, and pain. All the psychodrama you have experienced in relationships throughout your life will not suddenly disappear, but the significant difference in our relationships will be the additional presence, accompaniment, and guidance of the silent wisdom of Ourself. At times this understanding and guidance will help us resolve conflicts harmoniously, and at other times it will give us the confidence and strength to end abusive or destructive relationships.

As our awareness of Ourself deepens and spreads throughout our lives, we begin to ask ourselves, "How aware are we as we interact with others that at the ultimate level we are actually one thing interacting with itself?" Continually asking ourselves this question opens us up to the expansive thrill in our social encounters of being one aspect of Ourself intermingling with other aspects of Ourself. To approach this experience we must begin recognizing Ourself in others and simultaneously throughout our own thoughts and feelings. The transcendence of individual identity through the shared consciousness of our ultimate identity is the magic of being Ourself in relationship with Ourself.

Consciously being Ourself in relationship with Ourself not only transforms how we experience ourselves as individuals, but also further illuminates the nature of Ourself as a whole. This phenomenon is similar to the combining of unique foods and flavors. For example, we might be familiar with coconut combined with chocolate in desserts, but when we first taste coconut in a Thai curry sauce with fresh lime and cilantro we are introduced to a whole new delight as we experience coconut in a new way. When we remain conscious of Ourself in our encounters with others we experience new flavors of our own unique character through being combined with the distinct qualities of other individuals. As we begin to tap into this fluid nature of identity within Ourself we gain a greater appreciation of the immensity and diversity of Ourself, and we begin to move about in our interactions with other people with greater freedom and enthusiasm than we have previously known in our relationships.

When we come to recognize our individual lives as points within the all encompassing mandala of Ourself we really begin to get a feeling for the amazing potential humankind has to function harmoniously with the total community of Ourself. Of course the great challenge to human beings is that our minds find it easier to believe in separateness than to look directly at reality as Ourself. Because of our mind's capacity for identifying and labeling aspects of reality, composing ideas with these identities and labels, and then self-engaging in endless monologue concerning these ideas, we find ourselves living our lives as prisoners to the very rigid, limiting, and divisive framework of thought. Our thinking minds maintain a monopoly on our consciousness similar to the way in which the presence of a television can distract a child from a room full of interesting toys and books.

Within the framework of thought we celebrate and cling to our favorite ideas as our "beliefs." In essence, our beliefs are the ideas we have individually or culturally decided are the "right" ideas, and as a result we live in a world violently polarized along lines of religious and political beliefs. Once we have established our beliefs we unfortunately tend to quit questioning and looking at the nature of reality for ourselves. Living in the realm of reality is much more demanding to human consciousness than living in the realm of ideas and beliefs because Ourself is alive and always moving or changing, while our ideas and beliefs very quickly become dormant or static safe-zones rooted in the past.

Within these safe-zones our minds discover a perverse kind of freedom to delete certain obvious details or truths about reality. The detail or truth about reality that our minds seem to find *most* challenging to our ideas and beliefs—and therefore most tempting to delete—is the fact that everything and everybody, everywhere, is actually *one thing* interacting with itself. Our minds want to alter or ignore this fundamental quality of reality because the ultimate simplicity of oneness challenges the very mechanical course of thought which relies on separate identities and labels to function. Oneness is like the ultimate nebulizer to our thinking, as all of our conceived lines of distinction begin to blend and blur as we open our eyes to its brilliance and wholeness.

On the one hand it is important to recognize that if we don't think of reality in terms of separate parts we can not break reality down into mathematical and scientific equations for technological or medical purposes, or other productive kinds of problem solving. Our mind's capacity for such thinking is one of our greatest assets for survival in this world.

The problem, however, is that we are so easily hypnotized by our own mind's labeling and thinking that the true condition of reality's oneness as Ourself starts to seem like nonsense or fantasy. Now the challenge for us all is to look beyond belief, beyond knowledge, and entirely beyond the realm of words and thought in order to recover our natural capacity for first-hand insight into reality so that we can begin to remember and reclaim our fundamental identity, Ourself. As we become reacquainted with the one reality that we are all truly and totally part of, we need to adjust our knowledge, vocabulary, and thinking to better reflect our all inclusive identity, Ourself.

Just as a compass must be oriented to north to be of any use, our entire consciousness must be oriented to reality if it is to be sensible and meaningfully productive. As we develop the capacity to allow our thinking to function in its divisive and mechanical manner without losing sight of our true identity, Ourself, our thinking can increasingly be used as a tool that can benefit both ourselves individually and Ourself as a whole.

At present, however, most of us are living in total belief of the divisions and distinctions that our minds create, and as a result most of us have a great deal of difficulty in our personal relationships because both people in a relationship are operating on the false premise that they are two innately separate creatures rather than different parts of the one all encompassing creature, Ourself. Because our minds are not oriented to the oneness of Ourself, our divisive minds largely work against each other, and against the well-being of life on Earth as a whole.

Ultimately our human mind's stubborn insistence on perceiving ourselves and each other as totally separate is just as counterproductive to ourselves as individuals as it is to Ourself as a whole since there is no way to truly *benefit* yourself as an individual if you are simultaneously *harming* Ourself as a whole. This is why the hardest relationship we have to live with is perhaps our relationship with the great wholeness of Ourself because it requires us to widen our life's focus from our individual needs and desires alone to the needs and desires of the rest of humankind and the natural world. This is what propels most of us to remain stuck in the gerbil-wheel-like experience of perpetually avoiding Ourself.

In order to sustain this avoidance of Ourself we must have a foundation for the stories we tell ourselves, and the basic foundation is the fictional notion that somewhere in each of us there is a little thing we call "me" that is somehow in charge of our lives. What exactly this "me" is we never bother to really investigate. We then carry this unverified sense of "me" into all of our relationships resulting in an innate rift or sense of separateness from every person we interact with—even those we are most intimate with. In other words, we have the fundamental assumption that our relationships are an experience of, "I am having a relationship with you, and we are by nature separate," when the true situation is that we are having an experience of, "I am you, you are me, we are both Ourself having a relationship with Ourself."

Ironically our most nurturing and intimate relationships also tend to be the most difficult because the closer we become with someone, the more we are confronted by the limitations of our own self-identity and character, by the limitations of the self-identity and character of the person we are becoming intimate with, and by the sometimes intimidating common identity of Ourself. Intimacy becomes like a mirror in which we, at times, become painfully aware of each other's quirks and shortcomings against the backdrop of Ourself's unlimited potential for a kind of benevolence and sanity that is rare in any individual human being. With nowhere to hide we have to rise to an exceptional level of self-honesty and receptivity to work through the ensuing friction of intimacy. The rewards of course are well worth it—for only through rising to the occasion do we receive the opportunity to experience the profound sense of wholeness and joy which come about through being Ourself in relationship with Ourself.

Being Ourself in relationship with Ourself has a profoundly therapeutic effect on our lives because not only are we nourished by the love that flows so richly when we experience ourselves and another as one, but also because through this intimately shared self-awareness we come face to face with our own limitations; allowing us to begin the deep work of reconciling our limitations as individuals with the unlimited nature of Ourself as a whole. In the process we find that some of our limitations are outgrown, while other limitations we find new ways of adapting to and accepting.

When we find someone who is highly compatible with our own uniqueness, shares our understanding of Ourself, and desires and welcomes the coming together of Ourself in relationship with Ourself we are likely to feel immense gratitude and overwhelming love. It is a tremendous gift to have such a relationship or friendship, and only in this kind of relationship are the necessary ingredients present to allow our sexuality to blossom.

Sexuality without mutual awareness of our common sacred identity, Ourself, can be an invitation for heaviness and sorrow. Sexuality is perhaps the most profound opportunity to exalt in Ourself that humans experience in this world, and yet there are very few human experiences in which we are more vulnerable. So it is critical that we are truly safe to be all that we are as individual aspects of Ourself in any sexual experience we open ourselves up to. To give your body when your unique inner qualities as part of Ourself are not welcomed, heard, understood, and valued is a tragic contradiction that can only breed pain in the long run.

Of course it is not only our intimate relationships that require us to stretch or to grow in our consciousness of Ourself, but also our everyday encounters and casual friendships. When we engage with others as Ourself the basis and potential for true communion is always present, allowing for improved relations between not just individuals, but also between communities, nations, and even species.

Through our awareness of Ourself we can all engage in the practice common to most indigenous people of maintaining significant relationships with the creatures that are a part of one's natural environment; a practice which flows forth from the awareness that all creatures share the common thread of life — Ourself. We can all experience the nourishing intimacy of Ourself in our relationships with the plants and animals of the natural world, as well as with one another. Ultimately this is the means by which the total community of Earth will come into a state of true harmony and self-awareness as Ourself.

As we discussed in Chapter 3, Finding Ourselves in Ourself, an important indicator of what kinds of desires, talents, or characteristics we should work on developing is the consideration of how other people will benefit from our actions. In recognizing

Ourself we exit the realm of isolation, and enter the supreme company of *everything*. This shifts our focus from the perspective of, "How will I benefit?" to "How will Ourself benefit?" In most cases the manifestation of our best qualities will bring countless benefits to other people or creatures. In this way, our one-thing-vision will guide us into actions and interpersonal interactions which can truly be seen as examples of Ourself in relationship with Ourself.

Being Ourself in our relationships will also greatly enhance our capacity to be simultaneously flexible and strong in difficult relationships. Life inevitably confronts us with many challenging relationships, and while we may not be able to completely avoid conflict, we can at least learn how to better handle the conflicts that we must face with the wisdom and unity of Ourself.

Unfortunately there are many people who in their dark ignorance of Ourself are threatened by the powerful light of Ourself. As we make efforts to manifest Ourself in our lives it is likely that some people will try to hold us back. If we are to let the light of Ourself shine brightly in our lives we have to be coura-geously open in our feelings and our ways of being; even when others are critical, or perceive us as odd or weird. To sustain this lifestyle we must learn to stand up to other people who in one way or another attempt to keep us from shining too brightly.

Not only do we need to protect ourselves from the broad spectrum of dangers that exist in our relationships with humankind, but we also need to draw closer to people who share our one-thing-vision of Ourself so that we can support one another. How do we do all of this? At the extreme, how do we deal with people who do cruel things to ourselves or other people?

We can not passively allow ourselves or others to be victims of abuse or oppression. We need to stand tall as Ourself, and be ready to defend ourselves and others. In order to protect our freedom to manifest and benefit Ourself we need to take a careful look at a crucial ingredient to the interactions of people—power.

What is power? How does power affect our relationships? Do we find ourselves craving power over others, or are we more often oppressed by the power of others? Do we abuse what power we do have over others because we are frustrated by the lack of power we have in the broader world? How can we be free from our impulse to control others? How can we find freedom from oppression in our lives? What do we do when the obstacles to interpersonal freedom seem insurmountable?

To better understand how power is operating in our lives we must first look at our perception of the relationship between our individual selves and the rest of reality. Depending on our perspective of this relationship we will come to experience one of two very different kinds of power. The first kind of power, which we typically operate from, is the power of the ego which stems out of the perception that we are each inherently separate creatures. We believe that we are separate, and through this sense of separateness we find ourselves either exerting power over others, or being victims of other people's power over us.

The second kind of power, the power of Ourself, is of a completely different nature. This kind of power is *shared* power which serves the common good. It is available to everyone when we recognize that we are all Ourself interacting with Ourself. We can trust this power not to be manipulative or blind like the power of our ego, and in relationships where both parties are operating from this kind of power we can maneuver through almost any challenge or disagreement.

The problem is that most people are so attached to maintaining their ego-power that they will go to any length to stop us from functioning from the power of Ourself in their presence because they subconsciously find it so threatening to their perspective of reality, and their power as a completely separate individual. It is true that when you are being Ourself you are no longer validating the dominant consensual perception that we are each separate creatures in control of our separate

93

lives. With the light of Ourself shining through you, as it does through all of reality, you become consciously part of the oneness that almost everybody's mind is trying to deny or cover up. Therefore you—like reality itself in its wholeness—can end up being perceived as a psychological threat by anybody psychologically committed to avoiding Ourself.

Typically such individuals respond to this threat by acting out towards you, or at the very least putting up a subtle wall of resistance to becoming too intimate with you. The reason they are compelled to do this is that they unconsciously recognize the brilliance of the light of Ourself shining through you, and they want to flee its demanding implications which challenge their secure sense of individual identity. Therefore, to protect the unlimited self-preoccupation of "my, myself, and I," people attached to the perspective that everything is separate are probably going to attempt to keep you from being Ourself in any way they can.

This is why we must rely so heavily on the power of Ourself to give us the strength to withstand the force of others' attempts to force us to adopt or conform to their perception of reality. Similarly, we must rely on the power of Ourself in the ongoing struggle to fight against the oppression of others because we all have a responsibility as Ourself to challenge injustice as we encounter it, and to support those who face oppression of any kind.

The power of Ourself which we can learn to operate with exists when we transcend the power of our ego through recognizing the illusiveness of its apparent separateness. In yielding our ego driven power to the power of Ourself we are not surrendering our power to other people or to circumstances, but instead to the wholeness of Ourself. When we engage in relationships guided by the hand and power of Ourself, this shared power acts as a natural equalizer which allows for harmonious interactions because our human tendency towards either exerting power over others or accepting others having power over us is subdued or balanced through the magnitude of the presence of Ourself.

With this kind of power we really begin to have an opportunity to challenge injustice and oppression, and to work for what is right and true for the whole of Ourself. Most of us occasionally find ourselves in relationships, often with our own friends and family, that limit our ability to be all that we are finding ourselves to be as Ourself. When other people are trying to control who we are we sometimes have to take drastic measures. For the sake of our individual lives, as well as for the sake of Ourself as a whole, we must learn to stand up to anyone who wants us to be what we are not. Ultimately our freedom and health rely on our power remaining free and rooted in Ourself.

Sometimes we can affect some change by confronting those who are attempting to control us. If the person is honest, then a dialogue can likely lead to some changes. It might take a long time and a great deal of dedication to thoroughly explore the many seemingly trivial points of difference, but if both people are really honest, willing to listen to each other, and willing to share the power of Ourself, then almost any conflict can eventually be resolved. Sometimes it helps to have a neutral third person present, such as a mediator or therapist, to keep such a discussion focused, and to help ground the discussion in the shared power of Ourself. However, if one person is not honest, it quickly becomes destructive and counterproductive to even try to work through small differences because the person's lies make it impossible to ever achieve a state of mutual acknowledgment of the issues, which is the heart of any constructive effort to resolve a conflict.

In a similar vein, we each must thoroughly explore how honest *we* really are being with ourselves and others. We sometimes need to do a lot of questioning and critical reflection to find our own subtle wanderings from the truth. If we have been in the habit of altering the truth for most of our lives, then we might have a lot of owning up to do both to ourselves and others in order to initiate meaningful dialogue over differences. Though it is tempting to focus on the shortcomings of those we are in relationship with, we ultimately have much more control over ourselves, and so we should start by exploring all the ways in which we can increase our own sincerity and honesty.

Ultimately, however, we still need to hold others accountable, and eventually this can mean ending a relationship. Some people are just not able to be honest with others—probably because they are not really able to be honest with themselves. Though these people might not even realize the extent to which they are lying, and hurting other people with their lies, it is still our responsibility to confront their dishonesty. In an attempt to be sympathetic we can not sacrifice the truth. If somebody is unwilling to stop oppressing us, to stop abusing us, and to stop lying to us, then we may find ourselves having to completely disengage from whatever relationship we have with that person. This is the unfortunate state of Ourself at present—many people have completely closed themselves to the truth, and resultantly to real human kindness. While this tragic condition of humankind is difficult to accept, we can not allow ourselves to be victims, and so we must do everything in our power to stand up for and defend Ourself.

To fight for the true freedom of Ourself means to *be* this freedom, and similarly our relationships need to be exercises in this freedom. We need to be free to be sincere, or true to our nature as Ourself. By letting ourselves be true to Ourself we will develop into elegant and dignified creatures that are expressions of the highest qualities of Ourself. By nurturing and honoring this in ourselves and others we eventually shed negative relationships, and instead develop relationships that are open, supportive, and loving where the heart of Ourself pulses within the relationship.

Reflection 6

Stand tall with your feet slightly apart creating a strong foundation. Breath in deeply, and exhale slowly—abandoning the narrow focus of concentration for the wide open feeling that emerges as you lighten up in Ourself. Gradually consider the entire human race: the immensity and the diversity, the excesses and scarcities, the joys and sorrows. Recognize that all of this is Ourself interacting with Ourself. It is not an easy thing to acknowledge in view of the horrible violence and injustice that occurs daily, but the only way to begin the journey towards a lasting end to these horrors is through acknowledging the true situation that we are all one thing interacting with itself.

This acknowledgment marks the beginning of the real transformation of our current situation here on Earth. Though clearly beneficial, it is simply not enough for us to act charitably; for us to love our own family, community or country; or for us to work for environmental or social justice. If we want to really change the world we need to take the real *"giant step" for humankind— we need to consciously acknowledge and recognize that we are all Ourself.*

Having taken that critical step, reflect on the relationships in your life. Think of all of the people in your life, and how you feel about your relationship with each of these people. Who do you feel relaxed around? Who do you feel tense around? Who do you feel nurtured by, and who do you feel threatened by? Where in your body do you feel either comfort or discomfort when you think of each person? As the significant people in your life move through your thoughts and feelings in the illuminating light of Ourself, allow yourself to move and express yourself freely while exalting in Ourself.

Recognize the level playing field that all people exist on as Ourself. As you recognize that each person you think of is really

Ourself let them go and move on to the next, until every person you have circulating in your psyche has come forth and been recognized as Ourself. You need to welcome everyone into the true light of Ourself—both the people you feel good about and the people you don't feel so good about. Once their ultimate identity, Ourself, has been acknowledged, then let them go on their way. Like the musical number from South Pacific, *I'm Gonna Wash That Man Right Out of My Hair, allow yourself to wash EVERYBODY right out of your hair, and out of your body and feelings.*

In order to experience the real freedom of Ourself in relationship with Ourself, you need to accustom yourself to emptying your thoughts, feelings, and body of everybody you know in order to reconnect with your original nature as part of reality itself. Even the people we feel warm and fuzzy towards need to be honored and recognized as distinct aspects of Ourself, and not clung to like columns that exist merely to support us from collapsing. You need to become familiar with your primordial wholeness in Ourself so that you can relate to others as one whole aspect of Ourself interacting with other whole aspects of Ourself.

Don't hurry through this—give yourself a chance to really feel the presence of the different people who occupy your thoughts, feelings, and body. If we allow ourselves to honestly witness our inner workings, we will recognize several people within the framework of our consciousness that we are either comforted or intimidated by. Like Toto in *The Wizard of Oz* pulling back the curtain to reveal the little man operating the equipment responsible for the illusion of the big, threatening, green face of the "wizard," allow Ourself to unveil the significant players holding powerful positions in your consciousness. By gaining insight into who's there and how they are affecting your life you are taking the first step towards healthy differentiation.

In the very recognition of the enmeshed psychological relationships you have with certain people you begin to spontaneously become disentangled. Don't confuse this with becoming distant from the people you cherish and love—by honoring these individuals' distinctness and wholeness within Ourself, and also your own, you are not distancing yourself from them, but instead you are distancing yourself from your distorting images, memories, and ideas of who they are. This actually allows you to become closer with the real person in the here and now of Ourself. The goal is to begin seeing others as whole aspects of Ourself, and yourself as a whole aspect of Ourself; it is only through such wholeness as individuals that two people can experience the full range of intimacy of Ourself in relationship with Ourself.

As long as significant people in your life remain unconsciously in the shadows of your feelings or clawed onto your back you will never be able to totally stand up freely as Ourself and make your life really happen. By allowing your consciousness to be combed through by the pure inner motion of Ourself, the kinks that exist as a result of your relationships with certain people will be revealed so that they can be worked through.

The only authority in your consciousness should be your own awareness of Ourself—no person should be allowed to block the light of Ourself from shining directly through you. Rise up and reclaim your sacred wholeness as Ourself, and refuse to allow others to steer your life in directions that contradict who you really are! Similarly, honor all the people in your life as parts of Ourself, and surrender your desire or impulse to control their lives. In reclaiming your true nature you will be in a position to draw close to other people who are similarly in touch with their true nature. Then you will have the opportunity to really experience the bliss of being Ourself in relationship with Ourself.

Living in the world as it is, and studying the bizarre history of humanity, one wonders, "If Ourself is infinite and unconditional love, then how could it have created or formed itself into this crazy world that is so full of conflict, violence, and suffering?" What we need to realize is that just because our minds have the ability to ask this kind of question it does not mean that our minds have the capacity to understand the answer. The silent answer of Ourself to all of our questions is an eternal presence that the mind can not translate into words. The only way we can possibly accept or come to terms with the often tragic nature of reality is to surrender our mind's insistence on knowing "why."

If we can let go of this insistence, and become intimate with Ourself, then through this deep and intimate awareness of Ourself we will begin to understand with a part of ourselves that both permeates and transcends our thinking minds. There really is an answer to all of our questions, but we need to begin to learn the wordless language of the soul of Ourself to understand it. The more we understand Ourself's silent and boundless answer, the easier we will find it to begin to let go of our mind's expectation that everything should inherently make sense or be "fair."

As we open ourselves up to a broader understanding and perception of Ourself, we will see that within the conflict and craziness of this world there is a light. As we recognize this light we will be inspired to share it to encourage and support each other as parts of Ourself. The light of Ourself which can sustain and comfort us through the suffering we endure as human beings does not answer to the petulant demands of our mind for a neat rhyme and reason to everything that happens in life.

Rhymes and reasons are the stuff of our mechanical dualistic thinking, not of reality. Through the infinitely broad consciousness and identity Ourself we can gradually begin to accept that people and reality as a whole are not going to constantly conform to our expectations. While there is a fad which claims that we are in control of *everything* in our lives—that through our thoughts and feelings we attract all the experiences we have in our lives to ourselves—this theory begins to seem pretty ragged when you start to apply it to child victims of sexual assault, political prisoners violently persecuted for their positive humanitarian visions of a better future for all, victims of natural disasters, or individuals suffering from genetically heritable diseases.

While it appears obvious that having a positive outlook and manifesting love and kindness are ways in which we can maximize the positive qualities and experiences of our lives, it appears equally clear that conflict and suffering are unavoidable aspects of Ourself which exist at every level of the natural world—from microbiology, to the relentless competition of plants and trees for light, to the savage hunting of predators. All of this is Ourself in relationship with Ourself.

If we expect life to always be nice and neat we are setting ourselves up for continual disappointment. Besides, what would our lives be without the growth that we experience through the fascinating assortment of struggles we are each handed to work through? There are quite a few fairy tales that illustrate what people who grow up without adversity turn out like, and I'm sure you know a few such people yourself—individuals who are completely unable to empathize with the struggles of others.

Life is not always nice, and it is absurd for any of us to preach to others—especially in the face of tragedy and personal suffering—such catch phrases as, "there are no accidents," "everything happens for a reason," or "everything that happens to us we attract to ourselves." Whether or not there is an obvious thread of truth in such statements, it is clearly a very incomplete thread that we need to understand both the place of, and limits of, through the eyes of Ourself.

If things are going our way it may seem appealing to take full credit; either through identifying our hard work, our positive visualization, good feng-shui, or good karma as the source of our fortune. Such concepts of meritocracy (the notion that people reap exactly what they sow) validate our sensation of inherent separateness by helping us to feel like we have autonomous control, and are solely responsible for the blessings in our lives. In the same vein assumptions of meritocracy allow us to blame the victims of misfortune so that we are absolved from the tug of our conscience to feel compassion, or to try to help as we witness the suffering of others.

When tragedy hits *our own* lives we realize that these self-important theories no longer hold water. When we are the victim it no longer seems like our suffering is merely the result of our own laziness, negative thinking, or bad karma. What did all the mothers of Hiroshima and Nagasaki do to bring atomic bombs down upon their babies and themselves? In 2005, what did the people of the city of New Orleans, or the people living in the parts of Southeast Asia hit by the Tsunami do to invite such devastation to their lives through the destructive power of water? Were all good natured, positive thinking, hardworking, and therefore supposedly deserving people warned by divine providence so that they could build arks like Noah? We like to tell ourselves stories about why the world works the way it works, but such oversimplified stories or "truths" are inevitably deficient.

Nuggets of supposed wisdom are like arrows—any arrow of truth that is shot from a bow rises, has a brief moment of glory, and then falls to the ground. This is why no matter how many wise quotes we gather on our refrigerators we are still confronted every day by new challenges and complexities which require us to rise above and beyond the territory of the known, which is of the past, and to engage in a silent dialogue with the living whole being that we are all part of, Ourself, in the present, as we struggle to genuinely understand and move forward.

While it is obviously important for each of us to be honest with ourselves about the ways in which our attitudes and behaviors do influence our fortune either positively or negatively so that we can change and grow in ways that better our lives, it is foolish to think that any of us can be completely exempt from experiencing sickness or tragedy through any action, remedy, or wisdom. If we look at the lives of people such as Martin Luther King, Gandhi, or Princess Diana it becomes clear that there is not a direct correlation between maintaining an incredibly positive vision in the face of extreme adversity and attracting strictly positive experiences as a result.

Historically and presently, the consistent consequence of being a saint—in the sense of being an individual who stands up to ignorance and injustice to make the world a better place for others—has been persecution of one sort or another. It therefore seems naïve and simplistic to think that reality conforms to the kind of black and white laws of meritocracy, karma, or attraction that our limited minds, which base everything on the assumption of our innately separate existence, so readily conceive of.

Accepting the limitations of the isolating and polarizing structure of our thinking minds, we can begin to embrace reality itself. Ourself is an all encompassing process of movement and change where we as individuals consistently experience the often painful bliss of inner transformation through the friction of hardship and conflict. Difference, confrontation, and conflict are integral parts of the story of Ourself; as are the delights of serendipity, synchronicity, love, and kindness. The wholeness of Ourself relies upon all of these elements, both the appealing and the unappealing, to propel itself into its infinite variety of characters and characteristics.

It is important to be alert to this in order to avoid being shocked by bumps in the road of life, and also so that we can proactively use all the very real power we do have to influence and shape the circumstances of our lives in the most positive way. Seeing the beauty of kindness and harmony, we will hopefully embody these qualities whenever possible, but we need to be equally ready to be firm Ourself-advocates in order to protect ourselves and others who are vulnerable. To protect our freedom to manifest and exalt in Ourself, we need to be ready to support and defend ourselves. We can't get away from the fact that conflict is an inevitable result of Ourself having manifested itself into distinct forms, but what we can hope and strive for is developing our capacity to resolve conflicts in creative, nonviolent, and mutually beneficial ways through the guidance and wisdom of our common identity, Ourself.

Just as important as our willingness to defend and protect Ourself is our readiness to love and nurture as Ourself whenever we are given the gift of such opportunities. We are each like a lighthouse. We exist in part to shine the light of Ourself on one another. Sometimes it seems like particularly bright lighthouses are spread out so that there will be enough light everywhere. This is why within every group you meet a few people who stand out as being especially vibrant or full of the light of Ourself. It can be lonely to be a uniquely bright light in isolation, but every now and then you encounter a kindred spirit and it reminds you that there are others out there shining the light of Ourself as brightly as they possibly can, living the unique life that flows forth from Ourself.

The more committed we are to being Ourself in relationship with Ourself in all of our relationships, the richer the rewards will be in both our already established relationships, and in our relationships to come. This is the framework within which we will find ourselves regularly meeting and befriending real "soul mates;" I say "soul mates" plural because when you operate as Ourself in relationship with Ourself you find that a wide array of incredibly rich and brilliant connections and relationships with others will start to be the norm rather than the exception. In other words, not only will you increase your chances of finding a truly compatible lover or life partner, but also more compatible friends, coworkers, and acquaintances. Additionally, you will find that the insights made available through your awareness of everyone and everything as Ourself will also prove invaluable in your more difficult relationships. It is only through our willingness to recognize the one-thing-vision of Ourself during all of our inter-actions with people that we begin the real march for peace and freedom in the world.

Chapter 7

Forgiving Ourself

The inner freedom we experience as we begin to recognize that everything is one thing interacting with itself opens us up to a profound new kind of forgiveness. This forgiveness which flows out of the one-thing-vision of Ourself exposes us to new ways of perceiving and understanding the painful experiences we go through in life. While recognizing Ourself may not allow us to completely escape suffering, it certainly helps us to develop a deeper capacity for forgiveness as we wriggle through life's ups and downs. This newfound depth of forgiveness is equally applicable towards other people, towards ourselves as individuals, and towards Ourself as a whole.

In essence, when we recognize that everything is Ourself we are propelled out of the victim mindset because it no longer makes sense. This is not to deny that tragic events occur every day in the world, or that many of these tragic events are the result of mean and purposeful actions, but instead to point out that there is a different kind of possibility for insight when we experience the tragedies of life as Ourself interacting with Ourself.

If we look at the different ways we all suffer we can see that some suffering results from accidental circumstances (like natural disasters or car accidents), some suffering results from the actions of other people, and still other kinds of suffering result from our own thinking, decisions, or actions. In regards to accidental circumstances, there are clearly many theories about why things happen the way they do, but ultimately life remains mysterious. All we can really do is be Ourself, recognize that everything else is Ourself, and trust that understanding and solace will reveal themselves gradually—often in non-verbal or intuitive ways.

In regards to suffering that comes about through the actions of other people, and also suffering that comes about through our own thinking, decisions, or actions, the fundamental insight that helps us to forgive others and ourselves is the recognition that the precursor to all harmful actions is *ignorance*—from the smallest misdeeds to the largest cases of organized genocide, somebody somewhere is in the dumb-zone. The perpetrator might be a genius in multiple ways, but the part of them that has decided to ignore the truth of Ourself and harm another person is DUMB—difficult to accept that we all have dumb parts perhaps, but unavoidably obvious nonetheless.

In order to proceed with a harmful action towards another person, we must be sufficiently shortsighted to miss the obvious fact that harming someone is not only going to ruin the victim's day, it is also going to make us feel awful. It seems unlikely that any of us has gone her or his whole life without committing some sort of jealous, petty, or mean-spirited act, and therefore it seems safe to assume that we all have had moments of ignorance where we clung to the dumb-zone just long enough to commit a harmful act. We are each parts of Ourself which have the capacity to ignore that we are all Ourself, and to act out towards one another from the ignorant and misguided perspective of "me, myself, and I."

Recognizing this does not eliminate the pain of the victim, or the pain and shame of the perpetrator once he or she has completed the act and is suddenly pushed out of the dumb-zone into the "oh-yeah"-zone. It happens. So what do we do about it? This is where forgiving Ourself comes in.

The forgiveness that flows so readily from the one-thing-vision of Ourself is not a naïve forgiveness. By being Ourself we will not excuse others or ourselves from accountability, or blindly put ourselves in situations where we are likely to be taken advantage of. Instead we will understand our own and other people's motivations better—especially the ignorance and shortsightedness of "me, myself, and I" that are integral to such motivations—allowing us to simultaneously forgive and protect ourselves by taking whatever actions appear necessary.

It is hard to forgive when we are repeatedly being re-injured by someone, so we need to make practical changes to protect ourselves from further harm. If we are the ones who are harming others, then we also need to make practical changes to protect these people from ourselves. Once measures have been taken to prevent further harm, then we can begin the freeing and lightening journey of forgiveness.

Unfortunately, there are a great number of situations where people being harmed have no way to alter the situation. Many people are unaware that there are far more children, women, and men in slavery, poverty, and oppression today then at any other time in history. Therefore, it is the duty of all of us as Ourself to be proactive in whatever ways we can to not only protect ourselves, but to also protect those less fortunate than ourselves.

As we become conscious of the absurdity of the never-ending monologues in our own minds, and how far our thoughts routinely take us from what really is, we might feel a bit of embarrassment or shame for having been so trapped by the inherent narrowness of the "me, myself, and I" façade for most of our lives. As we encounter this shame we need to approach our thinking with the same forgiveness of Ourself that we extend to others.

When our thinking mind is confronted with the awesomeness of Ourself that it is part of, it can respond like a scared, cornered puppy snapping and yapping out of control. We therefore need to allow the loving firm presence of Ourself to calm and sooth us with its wisdom, beauty, and forgiveness. Ultimately there is no difference between forgiving others and forgiving ourselves, because both processes flow out of Ourself's vast potential for forgiveness. This macro-pattern of self-forgiveness that the whole of Ourself exhibits is the model we all can follow as aspects of

Ourself. A crucial aspect of the great remembering of our common true identity, Ourself, is the ongoing forgiveness of Ourself towards Ourself in all directions.

To be a part of this we need to first recognize in every moment that we *are* Ourself; allowing ourselves to see with new transparency our limitations, shortcomings and flaws through the profoundly accepting and infinitely forgiving eyes of Ourself. Without this acceptance and forgiveness we find ourselves in a vicious cycle of psychologically trying to escape Ourself as we flee from having to look at our own limitations and our true relationship with reality.

What do we mean by escaping Ourself? Escaping Ourself is avoiding the obvious fact that everything is literally *one* thing interacting with itself. Avoiding this fact requires an incessant effort by our minds which will go to almost any length to maintain the illusion of separate identity. Our thoughts, conversations, and institutions all serve as co-participants in this massive escape from Ourself that humankind has been engaged in for as long as anyone can remember. This is really not a case of humankind running from something separate, but is actually a case of Ourself running from itself. When we as individuals recognize that everything around us and within us is all Ourself, we are actually reality reawakening to and recognizing itself!

This recognition by humankind that *we are reality itself* is long overdue, and we need to take a serious look at what costs to both the individual and collective good our escape from Ourself has had. The time has come for Ourself to begin remembering itself, recognizing itself, and being itself within us all. Imagine the kinds of sweeping improvements that could occur in this world, both for humanity and for the rest of life on earth if a critical mass of humankind were to remember our true identity, Ourself, and to shed the countless isolated identities we currently cling so desperately to.

Unfortunately, escaping Ourself is the pursuit most of us are much more committed to, and we therefore unconsciously support one another in this great escape. We try to escape the profound oneness that we are a part of because it has implications that we fear will obstruct our self-centered pursuits by causing us to reflect on our motives and priorities. As we encounter people with pressing needs, or plants and animals struggling against extinction, we want to be able to maintain our "space" so that our focus on satisfying our own desires and needs will not be interrupted. In general, we do not want to be aware that we are actually one with everyone and everything because we do not want to share in the suffering of others, or feel responsible to help others in crisis.

When Jesus said, "Love thy neighbor as thyself," he was essentially saying, "Recognize that your neighbor *actually is* yourself!" We are all inextricably the same one thing—the same substance propelled by the same source. So whether we like it or not we do have a relationship and responsibility to others. Rather than simply blaming people who are suffering as a way of trying to weasel out of our relationship and responsibility to others as Ourself, we need to begin acknowledging these relationships and responsibilities and begin to openly follow the guidance and insight we encounter through our awareness of Ourself concerning the ways we can help one another.

This guidance is crucial if we are to be effective in our efforts to help others. None of us is Superman; we have to follow the guidance of Ourself to know where, when, and how it is best for us to help so that we don't exhaust ourselves trying to help in ways that we won't be able to really follow through with, or that appear to us to be helpful but actually are insignificant or even harmful. In order to sincerely listen to this vital guidance of Ourself we need to be constantly working through our resistances, and exploring and understanding what lies behind these resistances.

In our great escape from Ourself we make an especially strong effort to maintain our separateness from those aspects of reality that we have the most resistance to: the chaos, filth, ugliness, and wildness of Ourself. We have created many variations of "sophistication" over the centuries which all have at their root an effort to circumvent the unavoidable messiness of life that we are so resistant to, but which is such an integral part of Ourself.

Most of the conventions of western civilization have originated as part of the great escape from Ourself in one form or another. We have our preferences, and in our pursuit of them we don't want to have to consider anything or anybody else—after all, "Didn't we already make a donation to charity this year, darling?"

We fear the intricately interwoven layers of responsibility we all have to the earth and its creatures—including each other—and all of this responsibility becomes undeniable when we fully acknowledge that everybody and everything is Ourself. Driven by this fear of being held back from our individual preferences and pursuits we have built a culture that values selfish individualism and hoarding above all else. Of course we occasionally throw in a little civilized charity in the mix, when convenient, to alleviate our guilt. The results of this overemphasis on individualism and our reckless denial of the profound oneness and interdependence of Ourself can be seen all around us in the form of violence, poverty, environmental destruction, stress, anxiety, and depression.

Recognizing Ourself is the way of transcendence out of this violent ugliness. In recognizing Ourself we encounter an authentic basis for forgiveness and transformative action. If we are ever to come to a place of joy and harmony in our lives, we must develop a forgiving heart towards the blindness and ignorance that has led us into this mess in the first place. It doesn't do any good for us to remain stuck in anger, frustration, or guilt about the state of affairs in this world. What *would* do us all a great deal of good is to begin to recognize our common ground as parts of one whole, and to share this vision with as many people as we possibly can.

As we begin to work towards this recognition there is a tendency to feel guilt or to blame ourselves as separate creatures for our continuously resurfacing denial of Ourself, but this tendency only further strengthens our sensation of separateness as it perpetuates the never-ending self-concerned monologue of our minds. In a similar vein we bash ourselves for not being Jesus, Buddha, the Dalai-Lama, or some other person we have attributed enlightenment to; again further strengthening and supporting the assumption that we as individuals have intrinsically separate existence. Some of us also attack ourselves for not praying or meditating more, as though there is some running tally of how much effort we put into "our" enlightenment. This too moves us in the opposite direction of enlightenment—every effort we make from the perspective of "me" to somehow lessen or transcend "me" actually only strengthens "me" as any action of thought is structurally tainted with the concept of "me." Trying to think our way beyond our thinking is like trying to fly by walking really fast. Walking won't ever allow us to fly and thinking won't ever bring us to that which is beyond thought.

This is the fallacy of "self-knowledge" or "self-awareness." Real self-awareness is the abandonment of our thought-oriented search for self-knowledge through the discovery that we are, and always have been, Ourself. In essence, enlightenment is the simple recognition that "me, myself, and I" are not something to try to get rid of, but are instead something to merely recognize as part of everything else that is going on within the one all-inclusive phenomenon of Ourself. The foundation for any kind of genuine self-knowledge or self-awareness is the recognition that no matter how unique our individual traits are we remain inextricably woven from the one yarn of reality.

How has humankind been so effectively duped into believing ourselves to be innately separate creatures by our thinking minds? How did we first begin to get lost in the sauce of "me, myself, and I," or begin taking the chatter of thought so seriously and literally? Just as we love to get lost in the story of things, which is why we love movies and novels, Ourself also appears to have an innate love of story and drama. Our belief in ourselves as separate individuals has allowed Ourself to indulge and engage in an amazing range of story and drama through us, and to thereby experience the sensation of being billions of different people facing billions of unique situations all at once!

At present it seems that the desperate state of humanity and the environment require Ourself to begin to move past this perhaps entertaining façade of separateness, and to begin remembering its true nature and identity. This means we, as parts of Ourself, each have to participate in our share of the remembering! Fully engaging ourselves in the story of our unique lives may be critical, but it is our secondary responsibility. Our primary responsibility is not to lose track of the whole—not to lose the true perspective that we are all Ourself interacting with Ourself. If we lose sight of this, then we no longer have the balance, security and freedom that come with understanding ourselves as part of the whole of Ourself as we approach the unique story of our lives.

As we are exposed to this ongoing realization of our true identity we are aspects of Ourself remembering Ourself. As we recognize our shared identity with all people and all things, we become familiar with the real compassion and forgiveness of Ourself. The time has come for us to quit denying our oneness, and to join in the work of rebuilding this world to reflect this oneness—to eliminate the poverty, cruelty, and destruction that are so rampant in the world.

The problem is that our digression into immediately forgetting Ourself is such a reliably rapid relapse! All it takes is one thought to catch our attention and swing it away from the balanced perception of wholeness, and back to the enticing polarity of separateness. Once our minds have cut up Ourself like an apple slicer the sanity and wisdom of the great wholeness is gone. Like magicians who are able to perform their tricks so slyly that most people are unable to detect how they really do them, our minds are able to engage our consciousness in a way that makes separateness appear valid, complete, or thorough so that most of us are unable to detect what exists underneath the surface of our mind's isolating labels.

This is why this book may seem repetitive at times—because the process of our minds escaping Ourself is so repetitive. It goes on all day every day for our entire lives! This book is a never ending cry for us to recognize the face of Ourself within our thinking, and to not be duped by the mind's constant implied suggestion that everything in reality is separate just because the mind can separately label things.

It is not only our individual thinking that deludes us, but the consensual assumption of separateness that society as a whole supports through its thorough and complicated systems of division such as individual legal rights, and individual property ownership. The pressures of daily life and survival as an individual constantly cement the sensation of separateness by demanding us to be on guard defending our rights and property. While we each must attend to our individual responsibilities, do we perhaps like to stay stuck in the details of our individual responsibilities in order to avoid having to face the big non-detail of our common absolute identity, Ourself?

Laziness and attachment to comfort, security, and pleasure are obviously considerable influences on our compulsion to limit our identity to our individual selves or immediate families. While individual and family identity may be important aspects of our overall identity, we must frame these within our shared absolute identity Ourself if we are to ever harmoniously engage in the broad and critical work of being Ourself.

Recognition of Ourself comes about when our passionate discontent with our experience of escaping Ourself reaches a crescendo. When we are literally starving for the truth, we begin to see through the toxic illusion of our separateness. This doesn't mean that we won't still find ourselves engaging in our divisive thinking, but instead that we will regularly be compelled to detach from the illusion of separateness by recognizing our thinking as Ourself engaged in the thrill of escaping itself, or playing at being separate from itself.

After all, we have to keep our individual lives thriving, and that takes some enthusiasm for our individual desires and pursuits. However, when we are aware that this process is all part of Ourself, then balance, freedom, and harmony become the dominant qualities of the unique stories of our individual lives, and we no longer suffer with the fundamental angst that is the inevitable and powerful result of escaping Ourself. Through the one-thing-vision of Ourself our inner lives become blessed with humor and humility which set the stage for forgiveness. What is called for is acceptance, but not resignation; forgiveness, but not naivety.

Realizing that we are Ourself transforms the rigid sense of individual responsibility which society teaches us we each possess. It is not that we are not responsible, but that we are responsible as Ourself. In other words, the locus of responsibility lies in the wholeness of reality rather than within some abstract center or core that the narrow "me, myself, and I" monologue of our minds supposedly refers to.

The sane approach to thought's conception of separate identity and individual responsibility is to allow ourselves to be humored by it in the light of Ourself. Through humor the thin veil of the self is lifted, and with it the weight, shame, and guilt of self-responsibility is shed. The one-thing-vision of Ourself awakens a much more immediate sense of responsibility that makes our idea of absolute individualism and responsibility appear absurd. To really be responsible is to be all that we can be as individuals developing our unique interests and talents, while simultaneously contributing to the overall workload and well-being of humankind, and planet Earth with all its creatures, as Ourself.

When we are in a state of obliviousness to our true identity Ourself, our minds are essentially parts of Ourself that are telling the lie that they are separate, and so there is an obvious fear dwelling in our consciousness as parts of Ourself that our mind's lie will be discovered. This is why we take our thoughts so seriously, and are so easily offended by anything that challenges this seriousness or our assumption that there really is a little "me" stuck somewhere inside of us. In other words, our mind is afraid that the false storyline of separateness will be noticed, and in the process of losing our cover we will lose control.

This is the real foundation of psychological fear. While fear is not necessarily a "bad" thing, the psychological fear that results from living blindly as a captive to the illusion of individual control is a destructive and limiting force in the lives of humans. Our instinctual response of fear in itself is healthy, as there exist many dangers in this world which we all must guard ourselves against, but fear of the oneness of Ourself somehow nullifying our individual identity and control is unfounded. While we *are* merely pieces of the same one thing that is *everything* thinking to itself and interacting with itself, we are also powerful players and contributors as individuals within the whole of Ourself. Recognizing ourselves as individuals within the true context of Ourself as a whole brings us *greater* clarity as to who we are, and having found ourselves in Ourself, we become even more powerful and effective as individuals.

Because our mind's misperception that we are each a completely separate entity is fundamentally incongruent with reality, this misperception is very fragile. Therefore, we live in a constant state of fear that our fragile, false construction of what we are will be shattered. If *we take the initiative*, and allow our perception of ourselves as separate to be confronted and challenged by the profound silence of the one-thing-look of reality, then our fear becomes obsolete.

Sadly, most of us don't have this kind of inner initiative, and so we carry this unconscious fear right to our deathbed. To make matters worse, this primary fear concerning the façade of our separateness being discovered is merely the hub or center of a wheel out of which come many spokes. While "me" is the primary thing we are afraid of losing, we similarly fear the loss of the many spokes of "mine"—my career, my friends and family, my property, my health, my knowledge, and my beliefs.

The effect of living with such an extensive fear of loss is that there exists for many of us a basic feeling of mistrust towards life. We want to be happy and to trust life, but there is so much suffering in the world that seems beyond anyone's control, and sometimes it seems like the moment we let our guard down and start enjoying ourselves life knocks the wind right out of us with unexpected setbacks, accidents, or bad news. When presented with the notion of the "oneness of reality" we ask, "If there is no separation between us and Ourself, then why does life have setbacks and tragedies? How can Ourself betray us by going against what we as aspects of Ourself want?"

What is critical to recognize is that Ourself is not an extension of our will and desires, but instead that our will and desires are extensions of Ourself. As we realize our will is not in control of Ourself we feel small and powerless if we are stuck in the misconception that we are separate, isolated entities. Fortunately, however, we really *are not* separate or powerless—we just aren't in control of the whole show. We actually have enormous personal power in being Ourself, but we aren't personally all-powerful. So how can we reconcile ourselves with Ourself in order to feel good about both the power we have and do not have as individuals?

Often the only way to change something about ourselves is to first accept that maybe we can't. The more we try to push away our fear, the more powerful it becomes; the more we try to be in control, the more we notice the ways in which we lack control. We have to allow ourselves to be what we are, and we are fearful creatures as extensions of Ourself because we are vulnerable.

Ourself is not a level playing field of homogenous and equally powerful parts. We do have incredible powers, but ultimately we do have limited control over each other and Ourself as a whole.

Opening ourselves up to really witnessing our psychological fear as reality witnessing reality is the way we can approach the deep acceptance that is necessary to free ourselves from the oppressive heaviness of our fear. If we could see beyond our fear of losing our individual autonomy into what really is, we would find that like the two sides of a coin, the flip side of reality is the enormous and warm heart of Ourself that pulses and breaths love, comfort, guidance, and understanding to us all.

To open up our awareness to this vast heart of Ourself, we simply need to soberly look at all that we have conceived of as separate within our minds, and to recognize these many different conceptions of people, places, events, and things as the mere reflections of Ourself that they are. Nothing can really be lost within Ourself as nothing is permanent or separate in the first place—or to put it differently, everything is always lost in the sense that nothing that we can think of or name ever exists in the permanent way that our thinking conceives of it. It is our mind's capacity to produce images and labels of things as though they are permanent which is responsible for our fear of losing such illusory images of permanency. When we recognize this we will find deep solace in the perpetual change of everything as one. Within this oneness we will become aware of the inner smile of Ourself that is the constant wind in the sails of all that is good, loving, and enduring.

Reflection 7

Relax. Breathe... Think of as many of your fears as you can think of, without resisting or criticizing them. Let them be all that they are. Feel all the emotions that accompany these fears. Recognize the common thread in all of the fears—your lack of control over the circumstances that you fear. We feel vulnerable because we do not in fact have separate inherent existence, and we do not have absolute control over anything in life.

Having recognized that there is no part of you that is in any way separate from everything else, allow yourself as reality thinking to itself to "talk" in your thoughts to the whole. Be Ourself confessing all the fear, anxiety, guilt, shame, and sorrow that you cling to as "your's" to the rest of the primordial whole of Ourself. This ancient process of confessing our troubles to Ourself instantly begins to lighten our feelings.

Now quietly ask Ourself, "If I don't have the power to control everything, then how should I proceed with life in view of all these concerns?" Listen… what do you feel?

If you open up and share what is really going on moment to moment in your feelings—asking every burning question of the soul as Ourself asking Ourself—and then you really listen, you will find that not only is your burden lightened, but that new insight and understanding will surface in your consciousness. In feeling and listening to the silent voice of Ourself you can begin to move through the issues you have been stuck on because Ourself's wisdom will provide you with just enough insight to take the next steps in your life. Ourself doesn't allow us to be gluttons for wisdom; we can't expect to be omniscient, but we can count on Ourself to reveal to our understanding what we really need to know to move forward.

Give Ourself the opportunity to remember itself, and to be free to live and act naturally in the form of you. Allow the bud of forgiveness to blossom in this freedom and remembered wholeness. Forgive not only all of the parts of Ourself that you have perceived as "outside" of you, but also all the parts of Ourself that you have lived with as "inside" of you throughout

> *your lifetime. All of the painful memories, thought patterns, obsessions, and desires that you have struggled with in painful isolation—let these come out into the light of Ourself as you recognize that they are all merely reality thinking and feeling to itself. Be Ourself loving and forgiving Ourself!*

If we take an extremely proactive role in our life, and do our best to develop and use our natural gifts and abilities to make the world a better place, Ourself will help us to make our way forward. No, we don't have absolute control, and we can not expect life to be snag free, but by feeling ourselves as extensions of Ourself, we can begin to regain some trust in Ourself. If we can expose the expectations, fears, and hurts that we harbor to the illuminating light of Ourself, then acceptance, humility, and peace will begin to dwell in our hearts.

When we have the misconception that we are separate fixed in our minds, then we feel betrayed and hurt by life as a separate phenomena that we hold responsible for anything in our lives that we are not happy about. However, in realizing that we are Ourself, we realize that there is no separate entity to be betrayed, or to be betrayed by.

Recognizing this, we move out of the victim mindset and into the mindset so eloquently captured by the Marvin Gaye classic, *What's Going On?* It is natural and inevitable that as we move through life, and are confronted by loss, tragedy, and injustice that we should wonder, "What *is* really going on?" Similarly, knowing that at this exact moment throughout the world there are people experiencing incredible extremes of suffering such as slavery, prostitution, addiction, imprisonment, and mental and physical illness, we can not help but to wonder "Why?"

While our thinking may not have the capacity to understand why life is the way it is we can begin to understand why life is the way it is through our feelings when we are conscious of ourselves as Ourself. Ultimately we are all Ourself trying to remember itself because as individual aspects of the whole of Ourself, we have forgotten our true identity.

The momentum of escaping Ourself, like inertia, wants to keep going. Because everyone is part of this momentum to keep emphasizing separateness, it takes a profound commitment to truth to recognize Ourself in every moment, and to proceed with building our lives from this awareness. We need to constantly be searching for the one-thing look within our thinking, within our feelings, within our bodies, and all around us, all the time.

Staying oriented to the one-thing-look of Ourself is a natural process similar to the way that we naturally stay oriented to up and down. Through thousands of years of psychological conditioning by the "me, myself, and I" process of our own minds, our assumption of separateness has shut down this natural function within our consciousness.

By regularly rising above the division and conflict of our thinking and recognizing Ourself we reclaim this aspect of our consciousness, and soon we find that what feels disconcerting and unusual is *not* recognizing the one-thing-look.

It is inevitable that we become regularly lost in the story of our individual lives, but it is equally inevitable that as our feelings become increasingly congested the heaviness will prompt us to stop and lighten up by recognizing the one-thing-look of Ourself within everything. This is similar to the way that when clouds become dense enough with moisture, it rains. When the heaviness of our focus on ourselves as innately separate individuals reaches an unbearable state in our feelings, something within us revolts against the limiting and isolating illusion of separateness that our thinking projects onto reality, and we remember that we are all merely Ourself interacting with Ourself.

There is important humility to be found in knowing that we are going to continuously tell ourselves stories—tales of division and separateness, with details that seem all important in the moment, but are like ashes soon enough. There is no reason to feel bad about this whole process. It is comical—the human condition is comical! We can not stop ourselves from believing in our mind's tales, and yet we are ultimately nothing but Ourself interacting with itself.

However, we do undeniably have a great deal at stake as parts of Ourself, and we therefore must give our all to the struggle to survive and thrive. We will never cease having to face difficult or trying circumstances, but it is critical that we understand these challenges in context, as Ourself exploring itself, if we are to avoid feeling hopelessly overwhelmed or angry. We have to learn how to enjoy the escapades of "me, myself, and I" like an actor engaged in his or her character, while simultaneously keeping sight of our true identity as aspects of reality. It really is possible to delight in our individuality while simultaneously basking in the great oneness that is Ourself.

Epilogue

Every Breath's Death, Ourself's Eternal Birth

With every life sustaining inhalation, comes a subsequent exhalation that peters out into the next inhalation. There is no exact line between the end of one breath and the beginning of the next—just a smooth and constant transition. That in-between space before inhalation and after exhalation brings to mind the space before birth and after death. What and where that place is we do not need to define intellectually, but it is important to recognize that our impermanent lives are framed beautifully by birth and death, just as all the moments of our lives are framed by inhalations and exhalations. These frames are reminders of the never-ending motion of Ourself, and of the impermanence of every manifestation of Ourself. If we can begin to see our lives framed in this way we will begin to value and treasure every moment of our lives as *the big eternal moment* of Ourself.

As each inhalation begins there is that grasping for life within us, and at the end of each exhalation there is that brief moment of the letting go of dying. With every breath we have an opportunity to inhale and make an effort in our lives with the full power of our will as individuals, and to then exhale and let go of the narrowness of our individual identity as we bathe in our fundamental identity, Ourself. This back and forth rhythm between being an individual, and being the whole, Ourself, is the lifelong inner dance of being human.

The problem in the world right now is that we have stopped dancing—we have lost the beat. Just like when the drummer of a band loses the beat, and the dancing audience stutters a step wondering where the beat went, humankind has lost track of the ancient rhythm between being aware of ourselves as individuals and being aware of ourselves as Ourself. We need to start feeling this rhythm and dancing again—if we do, we will find that this rhythm evolves into a glorious and familiar song. The apparent rift between being aware of ourselves as individuals and being aware of ourselves as Ourself will be transcended as we begin to be sustained by this song of Ourself.

When we really recognize that we are Ourself we regain our most important healing resource. On one occasion when I was having trouble with my phone line I was told to unplug the phone cord from the phone jack on the wall for a few minutes and then plug it back in. I was amazed after doing this to find that my phone worked again. Disconnecting the phone line allows some kind of buildup of static to be cleared so that when you plug it in again it works. This is the value of every breath's death. With every exhalation we can let go of the pent up static, anxiety, and frustration that have been building up in us through our preoccupation with the illusion of ourselves as separate entities, and the clarity of our awareness of Ourself can be restored.

The scene in the movie *Charlie and the Chocolate Factory* comes to mind where Grandpa Joe and Charlie are floating up towards a large fan because they have had a sip of an unfinished recipe of Willy Wonka's, and at the last minute when one of them accidentally burps they realize that by burping they come down a little bit. Little by little they are able to burp their way back down to the floor.

Fortunately we don't need to burp to come down from the buildup of tension that comes from trying to live out a life of separate individualism within the interwoven fabric of Ourself. With every breath we have an opportunity to let go of the burdens of our individualism, and to relax into our essential nature, Ourself. Each time you exhale allow the fragmented illusion of separateness to die to the truth of wholeness.

This is a good place for any of us to begin familiarizing

ourselves with the process and meaning of death which is inextricably woven to life just as inhalation is inextricably woven to exhalation. The process of letting the struggles and anxieties of our individual self gratefully die into the eternal song of our ultimate identity, Ourself, does not have to be a process which happens only once at the end of our lives—this is the essential process of being Ourself that is available to all of us in every moment. We can explore this process anytime, anywhere, and in the process our comfort with death and our overall serenity will both be significantly broadened.

Becoming familiar with the rhythmic nature of life and death helps us to become more comfortable with the rhythmic nature of comfort and discomfort, happiness and sadness, and receiving and loss. In other words, practicing letting go with every breath's death enables us to actually "get better" at letting go in general. This is not a form of self-hypnosis, but is, in fact, the exact opposite—it is the complete letting go of the self-hypnosis of "me, myself, and I" that most of us unconsciously live our entire lives as prisoners to.

As we experience the rollercoaster ride of both outer and inner circumstances we need to feel the deep and silent rhythm of Ourself to ground us and sustain us. If any of us thinks we can avoid the truth that we are all merely Ourself interacting with itself, then we need to remember that when we die we can no longer tell ourselves the yarns of "me, myself, and I" that we have been telling ourselves our whole lives. In other words, through death there comes a time when you can no longer remain duped by thought's conception of yourself as an implicitly separate entity—the jelly donuts will all disappear when your life reaches its end!

You can leave all of your letting go for that one moment of death—this image brings to mind those extremely steep amusement park rides where you feel like all of your insides are going to burst up through the top of your head as you fall—or you can let go of a little bit of your thought-manufactured bull&%@# with every breath's death so that the moment of your actual death will be just another awesome moment of being Ourself.

Step one is becoming aware of the awesome silent presence of Ourself that eternally permeates our thoughts and feelings, and everything else, everywhere.

Step two is beginning to carry this awareness into our daily lives both at home and in the world.

Step three is allowing Ourself to reveal to us our true capabilities and purposes.

Step four is beginning to take actions that help us manifest these capabilities and purposes as Ourself.

Step five is allowing ourselves to lighten up and exalt in Ourself, and through that process experiencing a profound cleansing of the toxic inner residue which is the by-product of a lifetime of belief in separateness.

Step six is beginning to allow our awareness that everything is Ourself to serve as a light within all of our relationships and interactions with other people. By allowing this awareness to come into our relationships, our relationships too will become exalted, transformed, and purged of the toxic residue that grows within relationships that have the assumption of separateness at their core.

Step seven is discovering the vast forgiveness that comes about as we begin to understand the dramatic tragedy and comedy of life through the holistic vision of Ourself, and carrying this forgiveness into every facet of our lives.

Now, enjoy being Ourself!

BOOKS

O is a symbol of the world, of oneness and unity. In different cultures it also means the "eye", symbolizing knowledge and insight. We aim to publish books that are accessible, constructive and that challenge accepted opinion, both that of academia and the "moral majority".

Our books are available in all good English language bookstores worldwide. If you don't see the book on the shelves ask the bookstore to order it for you, quoting the ISBN number and title. Alternatively you can order online (all major online retail sites carry our titles) or contact the distributor in the relevant country, listed on the copyright page.

See our website www.o-books.net for a full list of over 400 titles, growing by 100 a year.

And tune in to myspiritradio.com for our book review radio show, hosted by June-Elleni Laine, where you can listen to the authors discussing their books.

MySpiritRadio